REVISE AQA GCSE (9–1)
History
CONFLICT AND TENSION, 1918–1. ͐

REVISION
GUIDE AND WORKBOOK

Series Consultant: Harry Smith

Authors: Sally Clifford and Victoria Payne

Also available to support your revision:

Revise GCSE Study Skills Guide   9781447967071

The **Revise GCSE Study Skills Guide** is full of tried-and-trusted hints and tips for how to learn more effectively. It gives you techniques to help you achieve your best – throughout your GCSE studies and beyond!

Revise GCSE Revision Planner   9781447967828

The **Revise GCSE Revision Planner** helps you to plan and organise your time, step-by-step, throughout your GCSE revision. Use this book and wall chart to mastermind your revision.

For the full range of Pearson revision titles across KS2, KS3, GCSE, Functional Skills, AS/A Level and BTEC visit: www.pearsonschools.co.uk/revise

Contents

. . . .

A small bit of small print

AQA publishes Sample Assessment Material and the Specification on its website. This is the official content and this book should be used in conjunction with it. The questions and revision tasks in this book have been written to help you revise the skills you may need for your assessment. Remember: the real assessment may not look like this.

The First World War ends

The armistice was an agreement to stop fighting at the end of the First World War. It was signed between France, Britain and Germany on 11 November 1918, ending four years of war.

The First World War ends at last

- The war had dragged on far longer than either side had expected, and had caused huge damage to both sides. Eight million soldiers and eight million civilians had been killed. Many factories, farms and railways had been destroyed.
- Germany had defeated Russia in March 1917, and for a while a German victory seemed possible. However, this changed after the USA joined the war in April 1917 and the Allies made several key advances.
- Germany felt it had to end the war quickly and made one last attempt to win with the Spring Offensive (from March to July 1918), but this failed to defeat the Allies.

Germany hoped it would be able to keep the territory it had gained. However, the Allies insisted that Germany should accept the terms of the armistice or fighting would continue. Germany had no choice but to sign.

Why did Germany agree to the armistice?

After the Spring Offensive, Germany was short of manpower and supplies.

⇩

The USA was sending more troops and supplies, and it seemed to be only a matter of time before the German army would be defeated.

⇩

On 3 November 1918, sailors in the German port of Kiel had mutinied and refused to engage in a battle against the British.

⇩

In the following days, thousands of civilians took to the streets in Germany's major cities, protesting at the burdens caused by the war. Many German soldiers had been killed and civilians had suffered many difficulties.

⇩

To try to calm the demonstrations, the German chancellor, Prince Maximilian of Baden, persuaded the Kaiser to step down and flee to Holland.

The terms of the armistice

The armistice contained 34 terms. The main ones were:

- German troops were to leave France, Belgium, Luxembourg and Alsace-Lorraine (which Germany had held since 1870) within 14 days.
- After this, all German troops were to leave the territory on the west side of the Rhine.
- The treaties that Germany had forced on Russia and Romania would be cancelled.

- The German fleet would be seized.
- Germany was to surrender all its submarines, 5000 cannons, 25000 machine guns, 1700 planes, 5000 locomotive engines and 150000 railcars.
- All French, British and Italian prisoners of war were to be released immediately. German prisoners would only be released after a peace treaty.
- Germany would be blamed for the war and pay **reparations** (compensation) for all damage caused.

Reactions to the armistice

Britain, France and the USA celebrated the end of the fighting. Germany was facing the possibility of a civil war as the country was divided and in a desperate state. Many Germans were angry at how the war had ended. Many German soldiers believed the armistice was only temporary and that the fighting would soon start up again.

At the armistice, it was agreed that the peace treaty would be drawn up in Paris in 1919. The conference would be dominated by the main Allies (Britain, France and the USA) and the leaders of these countries had very different ideas about what should happen next.

Now try this

Write a paragraph to explain why Germany signed the armistice.

The 'Big Three' and their aims 1

In January 1919, representatives from the countries which had won the First World War met at the Palace of Versailles in Paris. The negotiations were led by the leaders of the most powerful Allies: Britain, France and the USA. They were known as the **'Big Three'**, and they had very different ideas about what should happen next.

The positions of the 'Big Three'

Prime Minister of France, Georges Clemenceau.

Prime Minister of Great Britain, David Lloyd George.

President of the USA, Woodrow Wilson.

Most of the fighting during the First World War was in France. France had experienced the most deaths and many factories, railways and farms had been destroyed.

Clemenceau was under pressure to take revenge on Germany.

He wanted Germany to pay to rebuild France.

He also wanted to make sure that Germany was too weak to attack France again.

Britain had also suffered severe losses during the war, and many British people wanted revenge.

However, Lloyd George thought that if the Germans were punished too severely, they might start another war.

He wanted Germany to be strong enough to trade with Britain.

He also wanted to protect the British Empire by taking Germany's colonies and by reducing Germany's navy.

America didn't see the need for revenge – it had made money selling weapons to the Allies and the fighting had been a long way from American soil.

Wilson was also worried that being too harsh with Germany would risk starting another war.

Wilson was an idealist and suggested ways to make the world better. These were called the **Fourteen Points**.

The Fourteen Points

Wilson's Fourteen Points aimed to encourage nations to work together. They included:

- freedom of the seas, which would allow any country to sail and trade wherever they wanted
- allowing countries **self-determination** (the ability to rule themselves)
- an end to secret treaties
- returning Alsace-Lorraine to France
- forming an independent Polish state with access to the sea
- the creation of a League of Nations, allowing countries to work together to solve problems.

Wilson and Clemenceau

Wilson wanted to focus on building a fairer world and preventing war. He did not want to punish Germany severely. Clemenceau wanted Germany to be crushed.

Key disagreements of the 'Big Three'

Clemenceau and Lloyd George

- Clemenceau wanted to reduce Germany's military so France could not be attacked again. Lloyd George thought that a strong Germany was needed to stop the spread of communism from Russia.
- Clemenceau wanted huge reparations. Lloyd George wanted Germany's economy to be left strong enough to allow trade with Britain.

Wilson and Lloyd George

- Lloyd George opposed Wilson's 'freedom of the seas' because he wanted to protect Britain's naval **supremacy** (Britain had the biggest navy in the world and controlled a lot of ports).
- Lloyd George also opposed Wilson's idea of self-determination, as this posed a threat to Britain's empire.

Now try this

List **two** ways that the British and French aims were similar, and **two** ways that they were different.

The Treaty of Versailles

The Versailles Settlement took months to negotiate. The treaty was eventually signed on 28 June 1919. The German people had hoped that Wilson's Fourteen Points would be the basis of the treaty, but in reality the terms were very different.

War guilt and reparations

Article 231 of the treaty was called the 'war guilt clause'. Germany and its allies had to take the blame for starting the war.

Article 232 set out that Germany would have to pay reparations to the Allies. In 1921, the final total was agreed – £6600 million.

Diktat

It was soon clear that the Allies were going to punish Germany. Germany was banned from the peace talks and, when it refused to sign, the Allies threatened to resume the war. Germany had no choice but to sign, and called the treaty a 'diktat' (dictated peace).

Territorial changes

The port of Danzig (modern Gdansk) on the Baltic Sea, and nearly 750 square miles of land around it, was taken by the League of Nations and became a 'Free City'.

North Schleswig went to Denmark.

Eupen and Malmedy were given to Belgium.

The Saar coalfields were taken over by the League of Nations for 15 years. The coal was to go to France as compensation for the destruction of French coalmines.

Alsace-Lorraine was given to France.

Poland was given land to ensure that it had access to the sea. This was called the Polish Corridor and split Germany in two.

Parts of Upper Silesia were granted to Czechoslovakia.

Run by the League of Nations ☐ Weimar Germany ☐
Transferred to neighbouring countries or annexed, either by the Treaty of Versailles or later

Danzig

Berlin •

Luxembourg

Germany lost more than 10% of its territory.

The **Anschluss** (union) between Germany and Austria was forbidden.

Germany's African colonies were given as **mandates** to the League of Nations. This meant that the League could allow another country to run the colony on the League's behalf. For example, Togo and Cameroon went to France, and German East Africa went to Britain.

The League of Nations was set up, but Germany was not allowed to join. This meant that most of the territory that was controlled by the League of Nations was effectively given to Britain and France.

Germany's military was severely restricted

☑ Navy: restricted to 15 000 men, 1500 officers and six battleships. There were also restrictions on the other ships Germany was allowed. No submarines were allowed.

☑ Army: The German army was capped at 100 000. **Conscription** (compulsory military service) was banned. Germany was not allowed tanks or armoured cars, and was not allowed to buy weapons. The Rhineland was **demilitarised** (Germany could not put soldiers there).

☑ Air force: Germany was not allowed to have an air force.

Now try this

The Versailles Settlement intended to weaken Germany so that it could not start another war. Give **three** examples of how this was done.

The 'Big Three' and their aims 2

Most German people hated the Treaty of Versailles – but the Allies were not very happy with it either.

For more on the views of the 'Big Three', turn to page 2. For the terms of the treaty, turn to page 3.

Britain (Prime Minister Lloyd George)

Aim	Evidence it was achieved	Evidence it wasn't
Punish Germany	• Many people in Britain liked the 'war guilt' clause.	• Lloyd George worried that the treaty was too harsh and Germany would want revenge, leading to another war within 25 years.
Reparations	• Britain received reparations, but less than France. Reparations covered 'civilian damage', which Britain suffered less of.	
Retain naval supremacy	• The German navy was heavily reduced, cementing British naval dominance.	
Trade with Germany		• Germany was crippled by the war and reparations – it could not afford to trade.
Protect British Empire	• Britain gained territory from the German Empire.	

France (Prime Minister Clemenceau)

Aim	Evidence it was achieved	Evidence it wasn't
Punish Germany	• Germany and its allies were made to take responsibility for the war – a huge blow to German pride.	• Many French people felt the treaty didn't go far enough – Clemenceau was voted out at the next election.
Reduce Germany's power in order to protect France	• The Rhineland was demilitarised. • Anschluss (union) with Austria was forbidden. • The German army and navy were reduced. • Germany was banned from having tanks, submarines or aeroplanes.	• Clemenceau had argued that Germany should not have an army at all. • Clemenceau had wanted the Rhineland to be independent, not just demilitarised.
Reparations to rebuild France	• In 1921, Germany was told to pay £6600 million, with France receiving the biggest share. • France got the coal from the Saar for 15 years.	• The reparations were far less than the cost of the war. • Clemenceau had argued that they should be given the Saar outright.

USA (President Woodrow Wilson)

Aim	Evidence it was achieved	Evidence it wasn't
Self-determination	• Small nations that had been part of Austria-Hungary became independent.	• Germany's empire was given to the League of Nations as mandates.
Prevent future war	• The countries in the League of Nations agreed to work together to avoid war.	• Like Lloyd George, Wilson was worried that the treaty was too harsh and that Germany would seek revenge.
Set up the League of Nations	• The League was created and 42 countries joined.	
Freedom of the seas		• Germany's navy was reduced and Britain retained naval supremacy.

Now try this

Look at the aims they were hoping the treaty would achieve.

Based on the information above, which of the 'Big Three' do you think was most satisfied by the outcome of the treaty? Give **three** reasons for your answer, with supporting evidence.

Reactions to Versailles: the Allies

Lloyd George, Clemenceau and Wilson had gone to Paris with very different aims, and the Treaty of Versailles involved a lot of compromise. What were the short- and medium-term impacts of the treaty for Britain, France and the USA?

For more about the longer-term impacts of the Treaty of Versailles, see page 9.

Britain

Most people in Britain felt that the treaty was fair, although many thought it should have been tougher. Britain's losses had been enormous – nearly every family had lost a brother, father, son or husband, and civilians had suffered food shortages – and most British people wanted Germany to pay. Political campaigns were based on promises to punish Germany.

The treaty was generally popular – the press declared that Germany would never threaten Britain again and Lloyd George was welcomed back as a hero.

Lloyd George

Although Lloyd George was praised for his part in negotiating the treaty, and had secured Britain's empire and naval supremacy, he was not happy with it.

- He thought it was too harsh and that Germany would want revenge, causing another war.
- He also thought the reparations were too severe and would damage Germany's ability to trade.
- He warned that giving German land and people to Poland would cause problems because the people would want to be German again.

France

France had been the worst affected by the war – most of the fighting had taken place in France, causing massive damage. France had also lost the most men. The people of France were determined that Germany should be punished. Some elements of the treaty were popular – the war guilt clause, the demilitarisation of the Rhineland, the return of Alsace-Lorraine and the control of the Saar coalfields.

However, many people were angry because they felt that their suffering was not being compensated – they wanted the treaty to be much harsher on Germany. Clemenceau was voted out at the next election – people felt he had let the Germans off too lightly.

Clemenceau

Clemenceau was not happy with the agreement.

- He was furious that Germany had been allowed to keep an army – he had wanted Germany's military to be utterly crushed.
- He had wanted the Rhineland to be a small, powerless independent state, not just a demilitarised zone.
- When the reparations were set at £6600 million, he felt this was too little – he wanted Germany to be financially crippled.

USA

The USA had joined the war in 1917, and the fighting took place a long way from American soil. Many Americans felt that the treaty was unfair on Germany and had led to Britain and France becoming too powerful.

Many Americans were **isolationist** (they believed that the USA should not get involved in foreign affairs). The US Senate refused to **ratify** (officially accept) the treaty, arguing that as it wasn't based on the Fourteen Points, it wasn't in America's best interests.

Wilson

Wilson was very upset.

- He was scared that the harsh treaty would lead to the USA being pulled into another war.
- Most of his Fourteen Points had been ignored.
- The Senate's refusal to ratify the treaty meant that the USA could not join the League of Nations. Wilson campaigned tirelessly for America to join until he died from a stroke in 1924. The USA continued to pursue its policy of isolationism for the next ten years.

Now try this

Why do you think the British people were more satisfied with the treaty than the French or Americans? Give **two** reasons for your answer.

Reactions to Versailles: Germany

The German people were unhappy about the terms of the Versailles treaty – they thought it was very unfair. The impact of the terms on Germany, which was already struggling, was severe.

Instability in Germany, 1918–1923

Timeline

11 November 1918 The Allies insist that Kaiser Wilhelm II abdicates. Armistice signed.

28 June 1919 The Treaty of Versailles is signed.

March 1920 A revolt against the government (the Kapp Putsch) is narrowly defeated.

January 1923 Germany misses a reparations payment. The French invade the Ruhr industrial zone, intending to take German goods in place of the money owed.

January 1919 The communists attempt to overthrow the German government.

11 August 1919 The Weimar Constitution is accepted.

April 1921 The German reparations bill is set at £6600 million.

November 1923 Adolf Hitler's Nazi Party attempts to overthrow the government in the Munich Putsch.

Germany in 1919

During the war, propaganda had told the German people that they were winning – defeat came as a huge shock. The Allies blamed Kaiser Wilhelm II for the start of the war, so when he was forced to abdicate, many Germans believed that the person responsible had been punished. They hoped that Woodrow Wilson's Fourteen Points would form the basis of the peace treaty. They were suffering food shortages and the economy was in ruins – with the Kaiser gone, Germany hoped for compassion from the Allies.

German objections to the treaty

The harshness of the treaty came as a shock to the German people – they thought that the diktat was deeply unfair. Although the government had no choice but to sign it (the alternative was a return to war), the people hated them for it. They were called the 'November Criminals' and accused of 'stabbing Germany in the back'.

For more on the terms of the treaty, turn to page 3.

The 'war guilt' clause was the most hated part of the treaty, as it was a huge humiliation. The loss of Germany's overseas colonies, large parts of its territory and the wealth of the Saar coalfields, along with the limits placed on the German military, added to feelings of humiliation and vulnerability.

Weimar

When the Kaiser abdicated, there was nobody to run Germany. A new democratic government was set up, called the Weimar Republic. However, Germany was in a terrible state and many people felt that the new government wasn't strong enough. There was also anger that not enough was being done to help people who were suffering.

The political situation was very fragile, with several revolts and attempts to overthrow the government. The Russian Revolution (the Russian Tsar was overthrown by communists) led to fears that communism would spread from the east.

Hyperinflation

Following the invasion of the Ruhr, the German government paid workers to strike so there were no goods for the French to take. They then had to print more money to pay the strikers. This led to **hyperinflation** (when money becomes worth less and less). By the end of the year, a loaf of bread cost 200 000 000 000 marks.

Germany made its final reparations payment in 2010, though it did not pay the full amount.

Now try this

Give **three** reasons why Germany objected to the terms of the Treaty of Versailles.

The wider settlement

The Treaty of Versailles was only part of the Paris Peace Conference – there were also treaties with Germany's allies. This wider settlement had both strengths and weaknesses.

Austria: Treaty of St Germain (1919)

- Land was given to Italy, Romania and the new states of Poland, Czechoslovakia and Yugoslavia.
- Austria was told to pay reparations (but the amount was never fixed).
- Austria's army was limited to 30 000. No conscription was allowed, and no navy.
- Anschluss with Germany was forbidden.

Hungary: Treaty of Trianon (1920)

- Land was given to Romania, Czechoslovakia, Yugoslavia and Austria.
- Hungary was to pay reparations, but the economy collapsed and so it was unable to.
- Hungary's army was limited to 35 000.
- No conscription was allowed.
- The navy was limited to three patrol boats.

Bulgaria: Treaty of Neuilly (1919)

- Land was given to Yugoslavia, Greece and Romania.
- Bulgaria gained some land from Turkey.
- Bulgaria was to pay reparations of £100 million.
- The army was limited to 20 000.
- No conscription was allowed.
- No air force was allowed.
- The navy was limited to four torpedo boats.

Turkey: Treaty of Sèvres (1920)

- The Turkish Empire was split up.
- The Allies took control of Turkish finances.
- Turkey lost all its land in Europe to Greece, except a small area around the capital, Constantinople (now Istanbul).
- The army was limited to 50 000.
- The Dardanelles and Bosphorus Straits were taken from Turkish control.
- The navy was limited to seven sailing boats and six torpedo boats.
- The Allies could keep troops in Turkey.

Treaty of Lausanne (1923)

The Turkish people were so angry about the Treaty of Sèvres that they overthrew their government. The new government threatened to go to war with the Allies over the treaty.

Britain didn't want to go to war, so agreed to a new treaty, the Treaty of Lausanne, under which:

- Turkey regained control of the Dardanelles and Bosphorus
- the limits on the armed forces were lifted
- some of the land Greece had taken was given back to Turkey
- the Allies withdrew their troops from Turkey.

Consequences of the wider settlement

- ✓ Losing industrial areas to Czechoslovakia caused the Austrian economy to collapse in 1921.
- ✓ The revolt over the Treaty of Sèvres, and the fact that the British agreed a new treaty with Turkey, showed that nobody wanted to use force to impose a treaty.
- ✓ Hitler and Mussolini knew they could break international agreements and nobody could do anything.
- ✓ Eastern Europe was made up of lots of small new countries.

Turn to page 8 for a map of Europe after 1923.

Now try this

Which of Germany's allies do you think was dealt with most harshly? Give **two** reasons for your answer.

The new states

The Paris Peace Conference redrew the map of Europe – with unexpected consequences. The Austro-Hungarian Empire was split into several new countries, which created fresh problems.

Redrawing the map of Europe and the creation of new states

Europe in 1914.

Europe after 1923.

The creation of new states

There were two main problems with this process:

☑ Many countries were eager to receive the reparations they were owed by Germany and its allies, and this put pressure on the negotiators to reach an agreement quickly. This may have made mistakes more likely.

☑ **Self-determination:** many new states contained people from different ethnic backgrounds, some of whom were unhappy to find themselves in a different country.

> **Self-determination** is the right of a country to form its own government without interference.

The new countries

Czechoslovakia

Czechoslovakia declared independence from the Austro-Hungarian Empire in 1918, and its status was accepted at the Paris Peace Conference. It was a democracy and it inherited much of Austria's industry and was able to build a strong economy. It was generally politically stable, although there were some tensions – a fifth of the population was German and many of them, especially those in the German-speaking Sudetenland, resented being part of Czechoslovakia.

Yugoslavia

Yugoslavia was formed from several different ethnic groups, and there was frequently tension between them. However, Yugoslavia remained relatively stable until its violent collapse in the 1990s.

Poland

Poland faced problems from the beginning. The Allies created Poland as a buffer between Germany and the USSR. Poland was given a strip of land called the Polish Corridor, giving it access to the sea while weakening Germany by splitting it in two. This meant that the population of the Polish Corridor was mainly German and hated being part of Poland. To the east was the USSR, which disputed the border. To the west was Germany, which resented the loss of land. Therefore, Poland was surrounded by hostile countries.

Now try this

Describe **two** of the main problems faced by new states created after the First World War?

The treaty and fairness

The peacemakers at the end of the First World War all had very different aims, and none of them achieved everything they wanted. But was the final treaty fair?

Evidence that the settlement was unfair

👎 The causes of the war, such as the arms race (where countries compete to have the biggest armed forces), were complicated and were not just Germany's fault. Yet the Germans were made to take all of the blame.

👎 The Germans signed the armistice thinking that the treaty would be based on Wilson's Fourteen Points – but it was not, and they were not allowed to negotiate. They might not have signed the armistice if they had known what the treaty would be like, and that it would be a diktat.

👎 Six million Germans ended up living in new – often hostile – countries. This gave Germany an excuse to reclaim the land it had lost.

Turn to page 20 to see how border changes influenced Hitler's aims.

👎 The new countries created by the Paris Settlement often grouped together people who did not want to share a country, which caused unrest. Czechoslovakia split in two in 1993 and Yugoslavia eventually collapsed into civil war in 1991.

👎 The Treaty of Sèvres was so harsh it caused a revolt and was overturned – this showed that the treaties could not be enforced.

👎 At the time the settlement was signed, many people – including Wilson and Lloyd George – thought it was too harsh and would lead to another war.

Evidence that the settlement was fair

👍 The Austrian and Turkish empires were broken up by demands for independence, which the Allies accepted to weaken their enemies. This meant that the agreement had to be made quickly to prevent instability – given the pressure they were under, the treaty was not a bad job.

👍 Germany had already agreed to several of the terms of the treaty at the armistice – including the payment of reparations.

👍 Germany only paid a fraction of the reparations it owed – and was able to rebuild its military and economy enough to start another war within 20 years. The problem wasn't the treaty, but that it wasn't enforced.

👍 The Paris peace talks came at the end of a war that had caused a huge amount of death and devastation, especially to France. Expecting Germany to pay for the damage wasn't unfair.

👍 It was normal for the losing side to be treated harshly. When Russia had pulled out of the war, Germany had made them sign the Treaty of Brest-Litovsk, which took away more than a quarter of their people and agricultural land. Many people think this shows that if Germany had won, they would have treated the Allies just as harshly.

Changing views on Versailles over time

In 1919, the treaties signed at the Paris conference were fairly popular outside Germany. Many felt that Germany deserved to be punished and needed to be prevented from attacking its neighbours again.

However, throughout the 1930s opinions began to change, and after the Second World War the peacemakers were heavily criticised and blamed for the conditions that led to war breaking out again. This is an example of how interpretations of events can change over time, especially when the consequences become clear. Being able to recognise why someone might have come to a particular viewpoint is a key historical skill.

Now try this

 Look at all the factors and decide which are more important.

Was the Treaty of Versailles fair? Based on the information above, give **three** reasons for your answer.

League of Nations: origins

The League of Nations was an international organisation that was committed to cooperation between different countries to promote international peace.

Formation

- The basic idea of how the League of Nations would work was included in the Treaty of Versailles. All the countries who signed the treaty agreed to follow these rules.
- After the dreadful losses of the First World War, international leaders wanted a way to work together to solve problems without having to go to war. The League of Nations was intended to encourage compromise and negotiation.
- Geneva was chosen as the League's headquarters because Switzerland had been **neutral** (not involved) in the war.

To prevent war

To resolve disputes between members

To encourage disarmament

The main aims of the League of Nations

To tackle disease

To improve working conditions

The covenant of the League of Nations

The covenant of the League of Nations was a list of 26 rules which set out how it would achieve its aims. The main ones are shown below.

Prevent war by:
- ✓ replacing competing empires with a world of independent nation states
- ✓ protecting the rights of individual member countries to decide their own futures
- ✓ protecting each other's territorial rights
- ✓ replacing blocs of military alliance with a new system of **collective security**.

> Collective security means countries agreeing to protect each other if they are attacked.

Encourage disarmament by:
- ✓ expecting countries to cut their military capability to the minimum necessary
- ✓ working together on disarmament to prevent a new arms race like the one that had contributed to pre-First World War tensions.

Improve working conditions by:
- ✓ setting up the International Labour Organisation.

Tackle disease by:
- ✓ cooperating with the Red Cross
- ✓ leading international cooperation to prevent and control disease (eventually leading to setting up the World Health Organization).

Resolve disputes by:
- ✓ replacing **secret diplomacy** (managing international matters by secret negotiation) with open discussion
- ✓ agreeing to **arbitration** (mediation to reach agreement) and legal settlement of disputes
- ✓ setting up a Court of International Justice.

Now try this

Write a short paragraph (6–8 lines) explaining the aims of the League of Nations when it was formed.

League of Nations: membership

The League of Nations had 42 founding members. It was dominated by the surviving imperial powers like Britain and France. However, three very powerful countries were not part of the League of Nations: Germany, the USA and Russia (which became the USSR in 1922).

Who joined the League?

When the League of Nations was founded in 1920, there were 42 member states. The member countries of the League of Nations reached across the world and included most of Southeast Asia, Europe and South America.

Most African countries were not members of the League in their own right, but were either League of Nations' mandates or colonies of European member countries.

To avoid another war

As a way to cooperate on issues such as health, trafficking and the drug trade

Why did countries want to join the League?

To have a say in matters like colonies or disarmament

To benefit from collective security

See page 10 for a reminder about collective security.

Who didn't join and why?

Some important nations were not members:

- The countries who had lost the war were not allowed to join, so Germany, Austria and Turkey weren't members.

- Britain and France were suspicious of Russia's communist government, so Russia was not invited to join.

- Despite President Wilson's key role in the creation of the League, the US Senate refused to allow the USA to join, fearing that it would lead to America being pulled into another war in Europe. This was the beginning of the USA's policy of **isolationism** (not getting involved in foreign affairs).

Changes in membership

Membership of the League changed over time. Austria and Bulgaria were allowed to join in 1920, and Germany in 1926. The USSR was admitted in 1934.

Between 1934 and 1935, membership of the League was at its highest, with 58 members.

Some nations left the League over disputes, such as Germany (1933), Italy (1937) and Japan (1933), and some were expelled, such as the USSR (1939).

For more about why these countries left the League of Nations, turn to pages 17 (Japan), 18 (Italy) and 22 (Germany).

President Woodrow Wilson visited Los Angeles in September 1919 as part of his League of Nations speaking tour. He travelled thousands of miles around the USA campaigning for membership of the League of Nations, but the country never joined.

Now try this

Why did the US Senate refuse to join the League of Nations? Why might this seem surprising? Explain your answer in **two** sentences.

League of Nations: organisation

The aims of the League of Nations were ambitious. It needed to be organised efficiently to make sure it could work effectively and meet those aims.

Turn to page 10 for the aims of the League.

The structure of the League of Nations

Court of International Justice

This was a court for international agreements. Any country could take an issue to the court, and a team of 11 judges and four deputies would listen to both sides and make a judgement, which both sides would then have to follow.

Assembly

The **Assembly** worked like an international parliament. It met once a year, and every member nation could send representatives.

The Assembly made decisions about membership of the League, membership of the Council and how the League should spend its money. It also appointed judges to the **Court of International Justice**.

Every country had an equal vote, and decisions had to be **unanimous** (everyone agreeing) otherwise the issue would be passed on to the Council.

Council

The Assembly only met once a year, so it couldn't oversee the day-to-day work of the League, and it couldn't react in an emergency. So there was also a council, which met more often.

The **Council** had eight members:

- four permanent members – Britain, France, Italy and Japan

- four temporary members (increased to nine in 1926) who were elected for three years at a time.

The Council could **veto** (overrule) the decisions of the Assembly.

Special commissions

The League of Nations also set up agencies to deal with major international issues. These included:

- International Labour Organisation (workers' rights)
- Health Organisation
- Disarmament Commission
- Slavery Commission (to tackle human trafficking)
- Commission for Refugees
- Central Opium Board (opium addiction was a big problem)
- Commission for Undeveloped Nations
- Commission for Women
- Mandates Commission
- Commission for Minorities.

Secretariat

The **Secretariat** was the League's civil service. It ran the administration of the League, and organised any non-military action the League decided to take.

How would the League deal with disputes?

Arbitration	Moral condemnation	Sanctions	Military intervention
Getting countries together to discuss problems	If one country was in the wrong, they would be told that they were wrong and warned to behave.	Member nations would stop trading with the offending country, in the hope that the economic impact would force the government to give way.	The League did not have an army, but it could ask its members to lend their armed forces to protect another League member.

> ## Now try this
>
> Choose **two** methods used by the League of Nations to resolve disputes between member states. State why these methods might be effective or not.

The League's agencies

The League of Nations wanted to improve people's lives because it thought that if people were happy, the risk of conflict would be lower. It set up agencies to work to achieve this aim.

The International Labour Organisation

Successes

👍 Got 77 countries to adopt a minimum wage

👍 Reduced the death rate among workers building the Tanganyika railway in Africa from 50% to 4%

👍 Recommended the end of use of poisonous white lead in paint

👍 Helped Greece set up sickness benefits

Failures

👎 Failed to ban child labour

👎 Failed to limit the working day to 8 hours

See pages 10–12 for more on the League of Nations.

Commission for Refugees

Successes

👍 Freed 427 000 of the 500 000 prisoners of war still being held after the war, and returned them home

👍 Introduced an ID document for refugees

👍 Resettled 1.5 million refugees from Russia

👍 Set up refugee camps during a war between Greece and Turkey

👍 Resettled 600 000 Greek refugees from Turkey

Failure

👎 In 1933, Germany vetoed an attempt to appoint a commissioner for refugees fleeing Germany.

Health Committee

Successes

👍 Sent doctors to refugee camps

👍 Started an international campaign to kill mosquitoes, which spread malaria and yellow fever

👍 Helped the Russian government organise an education programme to stop the spread of typhus

In 1948, the Health Committee became part of the World Health Organization.

Central Opium (later Narcotics) Board

Successes

👍 Blacklisted several large companies that were selling drugs illegally

👍 Introduced a system of certification for companies importing opium for medicines

Failure

👎 The Board didn't stop the sale of opium altogether – and some people said it was because key League members were making money from it.

Slavery Commission

Success

👍 Helped to abolish slavery in Sierra Leone in 1928, which led to the freeing of 200 000 slaves

Communications and Transport

Successes

👍 Introduced shipping lanes to reduce collisions at sea

👍 Introduced an international highway code

Now try this

Based on the information above, which of the League's commissions do you think was most successful? Write a short paragraph (6–8 lines) explaining your answer.

Peacekeeping in the 1920s

As the map of Europe was redrawn after the First World War, there were a number of arguments about where the borders should be, and some nations threatened to go to war. How did the League of Nations help to keep the peace, and how successful was it?

1920

Vilna

Poland and Lithuania were created after the First World War when Austria-Hungary was broken up. Vilna (now Vilnius) was to be the capital of Lithuania, but most of the people living there were Polish. Poland occupied the city, and Lithuania complained to the League. Poland was told to withdraw its troops, but it refused. France did not want to upset Poland, as it saw Poland as an ally against Germany. Britain would not send troops without support from other countries – so Poland kept Vilna.

1921

Upper Silesia

In November 1921, the League resolved a dispute between Germany and Poland about the ownership of Upper Silesia, an important industrial area. The Treaty of Versailles said that the population should hold a **plebiscite** (referendum) on whether they wanted to remain part of Germany or be part of Poland. Germany won 60% of the vote. Poland claimed that many of the people who had voted for Germany didn't live in Upper Silesia. The League was asked to resolve the problem. After investigating the issue, the League decided to divide Upper Silesia between Poland and Germany. Germany received more land, but Poland was granted the industrial zones. Although both sides accepted the decision, Poland felt it was unfair that a large number of Poles were in German territory. Germany was unhappy that they had lost most of their coal mines and, in 1922, the League gave them the right to import coal at a discount until 1925.

Åland Islands

In June 1921, there was a dispute between Finland and Sweden about the Åland Islands. They had been part of Finland historically but most of the population wanted to belong to Sweden. The governments of Sweden and Finland asked the League to make a judgement. The League said that the islands should remain part of Finland but that no military personnel or arms could be based there. Both countries agreed with the outcome.

Corfu

In 1923, an Italian general was in Greece, deciding on the new border between Greece and Albania. He and his team were murdered. Italy's dictator, Benito Mussolini, sent troops to occupy the Greek island of Corfu. Greece asked the League for help. The League ordered Mussolini to leave Corfu, but he went to the Conference of Ambassadors, a group of powerful nations, and persuaded them to undermine the League. Greece was forced to apologise to Italy and pay compensation. Satisfied, Mussolini left Corfu.

1923

1925

Bulgaria

In 1925, soldiers on the border between Greece and Bulgaria fired at each other and a Greek soldier was killed. Greece invaded Bulgaria in retaliation. The Bulgarians sought assistance from the League, which ordered both armies to stop fighting. The League ruled that the Greeks should withdraw and pay compensation. Greece was upset by this, as Mussolini had got away with similar actions in Corfu, but accepted the decision.

Now try this

Why was the League of Nations more successful in the Åland Islands and Upper Silesia disputes than in others? Give **three** reasons for your answer.

Diplomacy outside the League

In the 1920s, the relationship between France and Germany was hostile. German resentment about the Treaty of Versailles, the economic impact of reparations and France's invasion of the Ruhr in 1923 had caused tension to rise.

Locarno treaties, 1925

In 1925, Gustav Stresemann, the German foreign minister, realised that the tension between Germany and France couldn't continue, and he invited the French foreign minister, Aristide Briand, to meet and agree a treaty to improve relations.

In October 1925, Stresemann and Briand met at Locarno, Switzerland, and in December, signed seven treaties. Belgium, Poland, Britain, Czechoslovakia and Italy also attended and signed the treaties.

The conference was a breakthrough as Germany was treated as an equal, not as an aggressor. Many felt that it marked an end to German resentment over Versailles, and that it was a sign that Germany wanted to be a peaceful nation. The following year, Germany joined the League of Nations.

Terms of the Locarno treaties

- Germany accepted the borders defined in the Treaty of Versailles, giving up the claim to Alsace-Lorraine.
- All countries agreed to protect any country attacked by one of the others.
- France and Germany agreed to work together for a peaceful settlement of disputes.
- France and Germany agreed to submit all future disputes to an international authority.
- All countries agreed not to go to war with each other.
- The Rhineland was made a neutral region – no country could send troops there.

Kellogg-Briand Pact, 1928

Aristide Briand proposed a peace pact between the USA and France, banning war between them. France was still fearful of Germany and was keen to make other agreements to secure its national security. US President Coolidge and Secretary of State Frank B. Kellogg were not enthusiastic about the arrangement. They were concerned that the agreement against war could be seen as a **bilateral** (two-way) alliance and pull the USA into war to defend France if France was attacked. The USA proposed extending the invitation to all nations to join them in outlawing war.

In August 1928, 62 countries including Germany, the USA and France signed the Kellogg-Briand Pact. The pact was an agreement not to use war to resolve 'disputes or conflicts of whatever nature or of whatever origin they may be, which may arise among them'.

Locarno treaties: Germany had felt very vulnerable to attack by France since the Treaty of Versailles – the promise of mutual support made them feel more secure. The Locarno treaties were seen as vital in healing the wounds of the First World War, and Stresemann and Briand were awarded the 1926 Nobel Peace Prize.

Other agreements made outside the League included the 1922 Treaty of Rapallo between Germany and the USSR, and the Washington Naval Conference of 1921–1922, which agreed the size of navy each country was allowed.

Did the treaties improve the chance of peace?

Kellogg-Briand Pact: Although the Pact created a feel-good factor, ultimately it had little impact on stopping the rising militarism of the 1930s. It was also not what the French wanted – which was to pull the USA into a bilateral agreement.

Impact on the League of Nations

These agreements all involved countries which were not League members, so the discussions had to take place outside the League, making the League look irrelevant. This showed a key weakness of the League – important nations like Germany, the USA and the USSR were not members, and so instead of being at the forefront of discussions about peace and disarmament, they were not involved at all. The League began to be seen as a 'talking shop', where problems were discussed, but not where solutions were found.

Now try this

Give **two** examples of ways that diplomacy outside the League weakened the League's position.

The Great Depression

For many people, the 1920s was a good time – the end of the war meant that people were glad to have survived. In the USA, there was a business boom and lots of new jobs. The good times came to an end in 1929.

The Wall Street Crash and the Great Depression

In 1929, the economic boom in the USA ended with a huge financial crisis called the Wall Street Crash. (Wall Street is New York's financial district.) Stocks and shares lost their value, banks collapsed and companies went out of business.

By 1933, 13 million Americans were unemployed, and many had lost their homes. Many people were living in extreme poverty. This period is called the Great Depression.

Thousands of unemployed people queue in New York, USA, during the Depression in the early 1930s.

The worldwide impact

The Great Depression hit America, but its effects were felt all over the world.

- The USA had been an important market for companies globally – but Americans could no longer afford to spend as much, so profits dropped and unemployment rose.

- In addition, the US government increased customs charges on foreign goods, hoping to force Americans to buy American goods – this caused a fall in international trade. For example, the value of Japanese exports dropped by 50% between 1929 and 1931, which led to hardship in Japan.

- American banks had lent money to European countries to help them rebuild after the First World War – after the Crash, the banks recalled the loans (asked for the money back) causing huge economic problems.

The rise of nationalism

With unemployment soaring and people facing starvation, leaders started to look for solutions. Nationalists like Hitler and Mussolini became more popular by:

- promising state-run economies, providing for people's needs and guaranteeing jobs

- promising to take land by force to provide land, food and resources

- using simple solutions such as Hitler's 'Bread and Work' to appeal to people by showing them they understood their problems

- blaming other groups for their problems (for example, claiming that Germany's problems were caused by the Jews and the 'traitors' who had signed the Treaty of Versailles) and promising to deal with these groups

- promising to stand up for the country and restore national pride.

What did this mean for the League of Nations?

Turn to page 12 for the powers of the League.

The powers that the League of Nations had were ineffective against **dictators** (rulers with total power over a country) like Hitler and Mussolini.

These men were not afraid of using violence to get what they wanted. They didn't want to be bound by collective security and didn't care about 'moral condemnation'. The next step was for the League to impose economic sanctions but, in a time of economic crisis, most countries were not willing to reduce trade even more. The only thing left was to ask members to supply an army – but during a Depression this was an expense no country could afford.

Now try this

Give **two** reasons why economic depression in the 1930s led to increased tension between countries.

The Manchurian Crisis

One of the biggest challenges for the League came in September 1931, when Japan invaded Manchuria, a region of China.

Background to the crisis

Manchuria is a region in the north-east of China. In 1931, it was an important industrial area and other nations, including Japan, had factories there.

The Great Depression had badly affected Japan's economy.

The Japanese government was influenced by generals who wanted to make Japan strong again.

Japan had few natural resources – Manchuria was rich in coal and iron ore.

Why did Japan want Manchuria?

Japan had claimed Manchuria in the past – the Chinese warlord who ruled it in 1931 was weak.

Manchuria was close to Japan, and Japan already had troops (the Kwantung army) stationed there.

The Mukden Incident

The Japanese army, which dominated the government, wanted to invade Manchuria, but they needed an excuse to do so.

On 18 September 1931, there was an explosion on the Japanese-owned South Manchurian Railway.

The Japanese blamed the Chinese for the attack, even though they had set off the explosion themselves. The Chinese, understandably, denied any involvement.

The Kwantung army invaded Manchuria in 'retaliation'. The Japanese government wasn't happy, but the invasion was popular with the people.

Manchuria was renamed Manchukuo, and the Japanese put a former Chinese emperor, Pu Yi, in charge as a **puppet ruler** (a ruler controlled by someone else).

For more on the covenant, turn to page 10.

The League's reaction

China appealed to the League of Nations. This was a clear case of aggression – Japan had broken the League's covenant. However, many League members were reluctant to get involved. Why?

- China and Japan were a long way from Europe – most European nations had their own problems.
- Many people felt that Japan was entitled to Manchuria.
- The Japanese argued that China had attacked them first. Many people believed this.
- China was weak and disorganised – there was a feeling that Japan would run Manchuria more effectively.
- Some people in Britain felt that if Japan was going to expand, China was a more acceptable target than Australia.

What did the League do?

The League sent a commission, led by Lord Lytton, to Manchuria to investigate. In September 1932, a year after the incident, Lord Lytton published his report which said that Japan was in the wrong and should withdraw.

The League issued a 'moral condemnation' and told Japan to leave Manchuria.

Japan ignored the judgement and left the League. The League of Nations could do nothing – nobody wanted to go to war, and they couldn't afford to anyway.

The following year, Japan invaded the Chinese region of Jehol, and in 1937 began a full-scale invasion of China.

Consequences

The League of Nations had failed. One of the members of its Council had broken the covenant and the League had done very little, and done it very slowly. This showed that powerful countries could get away with aggressive actions and the League looked weak and indecisive. However, many people still believed that it would be able to deal with conflict in Europe.

Now try this

Give **two** reasons why the Japanese invasion of Manchuria in 1931 made the League of Nations look weak.

The Abyssinian Crisis

The League's reputation, already dented by the Manchurian Crisis, was damaged beyond repair by its lack of response to Italy's invasion of Abyssinia.

Background to the crisis

In the 1930s, Abyssinia (now Ethiopia) was an independent country, but surrounded by British, Italian and French colonies.

In December 1934, Italian soldiers clashed with Abyssinians at Wal Wal, on the border with Italian Somaliland. The League tried to intervene, but Italy's leader, Mussolini, had seen his chance to invade.

Abyssinia and the surrounding area, 1934.

Sudan · Eritrea · French Somaliland · Addis Ababa · British Somaliland · Abyssinia · Kenya · Italian Somaliland

☐ French colonies
☐ Italian colonies
☐ British colonies
☐ Independent

Mussolini wanted to add to Italy's empire – Abyssinia was independent so was an easier target than another country's colony.

Mussolini knew that Britain and France wanted to keep Italy as an ally.

Abyssinia had fertile land and good natural resources.

Why did Mussolini want to invade Abyssinia?

Italy already had two colonies bordering Abyssinia.

Italy had invaded Abyssinia in 1896 and been defeated – Mussolini wanted to restore national pride.

The League had not stopped Mussolini in Corfu in 1923 – he was confident it wouldn't interfere now.

The invasion

- The League issued a 'moral condemnation', but Mussolini wasn't put off. In October 1935, the Italian army invaded Abyssinia.

- The Abyssinians were armed with pre-First World War rifles, while Mussolini's men had high-tech armoured vehicles and poison gas.

- Addis Ababa, the capital, was captured in May 1936 and the Abyssinian emperor, Haile Selassie, was removed.

- In June 1936, Haile Selassie went to Geneva to ask the League to act.

- Italy left the League of Nations in 1937.

The failure of the League of Nations

The League had, again, failed to stop one of its members breaking the covenant. The League banned weapons trading with Italy, but sanctions did not include bans on trading coal, steel, iron or oil, which were vital to Mussolini's war effort. It was thought that the USSR and USA would probably supply Italy anyway.

Britain and France failed to close the Suez Canal, allowing Italy to send weapons and supplies to the fight in Abyssinia. They were worried that Mussolini would ally with Hitler.

In 1935, British foreign minister Samuel Hoare and his French counterpart, Pierre Laval, met in secret to come up with a settlement to offer Italy – the **Hoare-Laval Pact**. It would give half of Abyssinia to Italy. The plan was leaked to the press and Hoare and Laval were forced to resign.

Consequences: With Italy gone, the League was weakened further. Also, the Hoare-Laval Pact showed that Britain and France were prepared to undermine the League if it suited their interests. The League was damaged beyond repair. Small nations knew that the League would not protect them, and powerful nations knew it could not stop them.

Now try this

Give **two** ways that Mussolini's invasion of Abyssinia could have been challenged.

Outbreak of war, 1939

The League was unable to stop the increase in nationalism and militarism throughout the 1930s. The lack of resources and political will of its member states meant it was unable to challenge a strong country which was determined to have its own way – and in 1939, war broke out once more.

The USA refused to join, and other powerful countries (Germany, the USSR) were kept out at the start. Trade sanctions were ineffective because countries could still trade with the USA.

Diplomacy involving non-League members had to be done outside the League – weakening the League's position.

For more on why some countries were not members, turn to page 11.

Members of the Council would always act in their own best interests, even if this undermined the League.

Weaknesses of the League of Nations

The Assembly only met once a year, decisions had to be unanimous and the Council could veto them. This meant that decisions could not be made quickly.

Powerful countries were not deterred (put off) by the League's 'moral condemnation'.

The League did not have enough people to carry out its ambitious aims.

The League had no army – it depended on its members to supply troops.

For other challenges faced by the League, turn back to pages 17 (the Manchurian Crisis) and 18 (the Abyssinian Crisis).

The League's failure to prevent war

The Great Depression had made countries more inward-looking and less likely to cooperate.	Poverty and unemployment meant that people found aggressive nationalists, like Hitler and Mussolini, appealing. This led to hostility towards other nations.	The British and French were more concerned with keeping Mussolini as an ally against Hitler than in protecting the interests of the League.	The League's failure to prevent the invasion of Abyssinia showed Hitler and Mussolini that the League could do nothing to stop them.

For more on the Great Depression, turn to page 16.

For more on the rise of nationalism, turn to page 16.

Commenting on the League

It's useful to consider what people thought about the League at the time.

"If the nations want peace, the League gives them the way by which peace can be kept. League or no League, a country which is determined to have a war can always have it." (British historian Herbert Fisher, 1938)

"The League is very well when sparrows shout, but no good at all when eagles fall out." (Benito Mussolini, 1936)

"It is true that we have the League of Nations, but it is only a mechanical frame and the soul has still to grow into its body. The spirit of ill-will and distrust is widespread. Internationalism is only an idea cherished by a few and not a part of human psychology. Ten years after the peace, the sky is not clearer than it was in August, 1914. Europe has a million more men under arms than there were before the war." (Sarvepalli Radhakrishnan, *Kalki: or The Future of Civilization*, 1929)

Now try this

'The League of Nations failed to prevent war in 1939 because of weaknesses that were present when it was set up in 1920.' Do you agree? Give **two** reasons for your answer.

Hitler's aims

Adolf Hitler became leader of Germany in 1933, and his foreign policies were very different from the peaceful strategy adopted by Stresemann, who was foreign minister for most of the 1920s.

Adolf Hitler

Early life: Born 1889, into a poor Austrian family. Moved to Munich, Germany, in 1913. Joined the German army in 1914 to fight in the First World War.

Beliefs: Even as a child, he believed the Austrians should be part of a single German-speaking nation. Germany's defeat was a bitter disappointment and he believed that Jews and communists, who he hated, had betrayed Germany by giving in too easily.

Political life: In 1921, he became leader of a small, radical right-wing party – the Nazi Party. In 1923, he was involved in an attempt to overthrow the government – the Munich Putsch. He was sent to prison and while there, he wrote a book, *Mein Kampf*, setting out his ideas. Under Hitler, the Nazi Party grew stronger, and in 1933, Hitler became chancellor (prime minister) of Germany.

Hitler's aims

1 To overturn the Treaty of Versailles. Like most Germans, Hitler felt that the treaty humiliated Germany and that the men who signed it were traitors who had 'stabbed Germany in the back'.

2 To rebuild Germany's armed forces to make the country strong again and reduce unemployment. Hitler wanted to build munitions factories, reintroduce conscription and build an airforce (Luftwaffe).

3 To expand Germany's borders into the east to make up for the land lost in the Treaty of Versailles. This new territory in the east was called Lebensraum.

> In addition to his aggressive foreign policy, Hitler also promised to rescue the German economy by nationalising key industries and promising *Brot und Arbeit* (Bread and Work) to all Germans.

4 To unite all German peoples, whether they lived in Germany or not (known as the Volksdeutsche) and who had been split up by the Treaty of Versailles, into a 'Greater Germany'. This included the Anschluss with Austria.

5 To root out communism. Hitler hated communism and believed that it would destroy Germany.

> Hitler's German nationalism was deeply racist. The Nazis believed that the Aryan people (northern Europeans) were superior to other races, such as Jews and Slavs, who they referred to as **Untermenschen** (subhuman).

Why Hitler's aims caused tension

 The treaty was the basis of peace after the First World War. Overturning it would be admitting that the case for peace was flawed.

 Germany's armed forces were limited by the Versailles treaty, so rearmament meant breaking international law – and alarming other countries, especially France.

To expand into the east, Hitler would have to invade countries in Eastern Europe – an act of war.

It was unlikely that other countries would agree to give up their German-speaking areas, so this would involve invasion. The Anschluss had been forbidden in the Treaty of Versailles.

 The USSR's powerful communist government was building relations with Britain and France, and was an ally of the Eastern European countries Hitler had his eye on. He risked annoying a powerful enemy.

Other countries' reactions are explored on page 21.

Now try this

Give **three** reasons why Hitler's aims were popular with the German people.

Allied reactions to Hitler

Hitler made it very clear that he intended to rebuild Germany and that he was prepared to use military force if necessary. Rather than joining forces to stop him, other key powers reacted differently.

1 Hitler's aggressive speeches worried the British, but they were still scarred by the First World War and desperate to avoid aggression. In 1934, Hitler signed a non-aggression pact with Poland, which reassured many British people that Hitler did not really want war.

Britain

2 In 1937, Lord Halifax, a British politician, went to meet Hitler to find out what he wanted. The British prime minister at this time was Neville Chamberlain. He described his policy as **appeasement** – giving Germany a bit of what it wanted to avoid a return to war.

4 On the other hand, Britain signed the Stresa Front in 1935 to protect itself against Hitler. Politicians such as Winston Churchill thought that appeasement was a mistake.

For more on the Stresa Front, turn to page 22.

3 Appeasement was supported by many people in Britain, partly out of the desire to avoid war, but also because people increasingly felt that the Treaty of Versailles had been unfair and that Germany should be allowed to take back some of what it had lost. There was also some suspicion of Stalin (the Soviet leader), especially in Britain and the USA, and allowing Germany to become stronger would reduce the Soviet threat.

USA

The USA continued its policy of isolationism into the 1930s. The Great Depression led to very high unemployment (one man in four was out of work).	Franklin Delano Roosevelt became US president in 1932. He concentrated on tackling the US economy.	People in America were opposed to involvement in European affairs. In 1934, an opinion poll showed that 70% of Americans said that the USA should not have joined the First World War.	In 1936, Roosevelt promised to keep the USA out of war in Europe. He did try to stop Hitler invading other countries in 1938, but Hitler ignored him.	The US government did not try to interfere again, but it did start rebuilding its armed forces.

USSR

- The USSR was led by a dictator called Joseph Stalin. The government was communist, resulting in strained relationships with other countries.
- Stalin was worried about Hitler, because Hitler had been very frank about his plans to destroy communism and to expand eastwards.
- On the other hand, Stalin was also suspicious of the other great powers, such as the USA, Britain and France, who had been against the USSR joining the League of Nations.
- In 1934, the USSR joined the League.

France

- The 1930s were difficult for France. The Great Depression very badly affected the French economy, which was still recovering from the First World War.
- There were protests against the government and outbreaks of rebellion. This meant that the government, led by President Edouard Daladier, was distracted from dealing with the threat posed by Hitler.
- It was clear that France would need to rely on Britain if it was attacked.

In 1935, France and the USSR signed a treaty promising to defend each other.

Now try this

Give **three** reasons why so little action was taken against Hitler.

The path to war

Hitler promised to overturn the Treaty of Versailles and make Germany strong again. He soon began to rearm (build up a new supply of weapons).

Tension rises, 1933–1935

1933: Germany leaves the League of Nations Disarmament Conference

The conference ran from 1932 to 1934. Hitler said that he would disarm if every other country did too, but if they didn't, he wanted the same size army as France. France refused to agree to this. Hitler stormed out of the conference, blaming the French for blocking agreement. He then left the League of Nations, so he was no longer bound by the covenant and the commitment to avoid going to war.

1934: The Dollfuss Affair

Hitler was Austrian by birth. Like many Austrians and Germans, he felt that Austria and Germany should be united and was furious when the Anschluss (union) was forbidden in the Treaty of Versailles. The Anschluss was a key part of Hitler's plan to unite the Volksdeutsche.

Englebert Dollfuss, the Austrian chancellor, knew what Hitler was planning and because he opposed the Anschluss, he banned the Austrian Nazi Party. In 1934, Hitler ordered Austrian Nazis to cause chaos in the country. Dollfuss was murdered. The Nazi plot failed because the army supported the government, and because Mussolini moved troops to the Austrian border to stop the Anschluss. Hitler had to back down and pretend that the Austrian Nazis had acted on their own.

January 1935: Saar Plebiscite

Under the Treaty of Versailles, the Saar – an important industrial area on the French–German border – was given to the League of Nations for 15 years. Once the time was up, the population held a plebiscite to decide whether the Saar should belong to France or Germany. Ninety per cent of the population voted to rejoin Germany. This gave Hitler ammunition for his argument that German-speaking people wanted to unite with Germany. The Saar also gave him an important source of coal which helped him to rearm.

March 1935: Freedom to Rearm Rally

At this rally, Hitler displayed the weapons and troops he had been building in secret. He also announced the reintroduction of military conscription (all able-bodied men aged 18–25 had to do military service for two years). Hitler planned to expand the **Wehrmacht** (the armed forces) to over half a million men and build a Luftwaffe (air force).

April 1935: Stresa Front

The Stresa Front was an agreement between Britain, France and Italy to guarantee the terms of the Locarno treaties, prevent Anschluss with Austria and enforce the terms of the Treaty of Versailles. It did not seem to put Hitler off at all.

June 1935: Anglo-German Naval Agreement

Many people in Britain had felt for a while that the Treaty of Versailles had been too harsh on Germany. The Anglo-German Naval Agreement said that Hitler could build the German navy to 35% of the size of the British one. The British thought this was a good deal as it was fairer on Germany, while protecting Britain's naval supremacy. However, Hitler saw this as an admission that Versailles had been unfair and that he could ignore it. In addition, Britain signed the agreement without consulting France or Italy.

For more on the Treaty of Versailles, turn to page 3.

Now try this

List **three** ways in which Hitler broke the terms of the Treaty of Versailles between 1933 and 1935.

The Rhineland

Tension had been growing ever since Hitler became chancellor in 1933. The tension began to **escalate** (increase) when he sent German troops into the Rhineland in March 1936.

Why was the Rhineland important?

The Rhineland is the area around the river Rhine. It is part of Germany but it borders the Alsace-Lorraine region of France. The Treaty of Versailles had allowed Germany to keep the Rhineland, but not to have troops, weapons or fortifications (defensive structures) there, in order to protect France from invasion.

Hitler's policy of Lebensraum meant that he was going to have to invade other countries. He knew that if he did this, France and Britain would be very likely to respond – so he had to begin to strengthen Germany's western border.

Map showing the Rhineland in 1933.

Netherlands
Belgium
Germany
Luxembourg
Alsace-Lorraine
Czechoslovakia
France

■ German territory
□ Rhineland (demilitarised zone)

The entry into the Rhineland

| In 1935, France and the USSR signed a pact, agreeing to support each other against Germany. | → | Hitler argued that the Franco-Soviet Pact threatened Germany, by putting an enemy on both sides. | → | On 7 March 1936, 22 000 German troops entered the Rhineland. Many people welcomed the troops and gave them flowers. |

The Rhineland gamble

Hitler's army generals had warned that if France decided to defend the terms of the Treaty of Versailles, the German army was not big or well-armed enough to fight. His finance ministers warned him that if he failed, the fines that Germany would be forced to pay would ruin the country.

How did other countries react?

Britain: There was some sympathy in Britain for Germany – many people felt that Hitler was entitled to secure his country's borders. In addition, the Great Depression had hit Britain hard – there wasn't the money to get involved, especially as after the Italian invasion of Abyssinia, British troops were sent to neighbouring British colonies.

France: The country was in the middle of an election and starting a war would cost votes, especially as the French thought the German army was much bigger than it actually was. Like the British, the French had sent troops to deal with the aftermath of the Abyssinian Crisis and protect its nearby colonies.

Hitler grew more confident that he could break the terms of Versailles and would not be stopped.

With his western border secure, Hitler could now pursue Lebensraum in the east.

Britain and France started rearming and securing their borders.

Consequences of the reoccupation

Mussolini decided that Hitler was a force to be reckoned with and Germany and Italy signed a pact – the Rome-Berlin Axis.

Britain reaffirmed the Locarno treaty agreement to protect France and Belgium if they were attacked.

Now try this

Give **two** reasons why the Rhineland was important to Hitler.

Support for Hitler

Hitler knew that his policies would cause opposition from other countries. Throughout the 1930s, he tried to build alliances that would support him if there was a war.

Italy and Mussolini

- Nazi Germany and Fascist Italy had a lot in common but, in 1934, Mussolini had stopped Hitler's attempt to take over Austria after the Dollfuss Affair.

For more on the Dollfuss Affair, turn to page 22.

- By 1936, things were different. Mussolini's relations with Britain and France had deteriorated and he was looking for an ally. Hitler and Mussolini agreed that they would work more closely together. This was called the **Rome-Berlin Axis**.

- Hitler and Mussolini both wanted an ally in case their attempts to expand (Mussolini's empire and Hitler's Lebensraum) were met with opposition.

- In May 1939, Germany and Italy agreed a formal pact of 'friendship and alliance'. Mussolini called it the **Pact of Steel**.

Japan joined the Pact of Steel in 1940.

Mussolini and Hitler in 1937.

Germany, Italy and Japan are often referred to as the **Axis**. This name came from the Rome-Berlin Axis, and Japan was included when it joined the Pact of Steel in 1940. Britain, France and (later) the USA are known as the **Allies**.

Hitler and Japan

1. Japan and Russia had fought the 1905 Russo-Japanese War when they competed for territory in Korea and Manchuria. Even after more than 30 years, there was still hostility between the two countries.

2. In 1919, the USSR had established the **Comintern** (a group of organisations who wanted to spread communism).

3. By 1936, Japan had invaded a large part of China. The Japanese were worried that the USSR would step in to protect China. Hitler opposed the USSR and was determined to destroy communism. The two countries met to discuss an alliance.

4. Nazi Germany and the Japanese Empire made the **Anti-Comintern Pact** in November 1936.

5. The Anti-Comintern Pact was later extended to Italy in 1937.

Other potential allies: Spain

In 1936, a civil war broke out in Spain between the republicans (who were supported by the USSR) and the fascists led by General Franco. Hitler and Mussolini had sent troops to help Franco. This was partly because the communists were supporting the republicans and partly because it gave Hitler a chance to test his weapons and give the army and Luftwaffe some experience. Franco was delighted by the support. When he became the dictator of Spain in 1939, this was largely due to the help he had had from the Nazis.

Other potential allies: Britain

Hitler admired many British traditions and was keen to make an alliance with Britain. In 1936, he proposed a non-aggression pact. Many in Britain wanted to cooperate with Hitler to avoid war, but didn't want an official alliance. Instead, Britain strengthened its agreements with France and Belgium.

Although Spain technically remained neutral during the Second World War, Franco supplied Germany with weapons and allowed the German intelligence services to operate in Spain.

Now try this

How did Hitler's alliances strengthen his position? Give **two** examples.

Anschluss with Austria

In 1934, soon after Hitler became chancellor, he tried to unite Germany and Austria. He failed because Mussolini intervened. However, by 1938, Mussolini and Hitler were allies. Hitler tried again.

Why did Hitler want the Anschluss?

The history of Austria and Germany was interlinked: they had similar cultures and spoke the same language. Hitler had been born in Austria and he was determined to re-establish the Anschluss. In addition, Austria had an army and valuable natural resources, such as iron ore.

Hitler's first attempt to unite with Austria had failed. However, in 1938, he was ready to try again.

For more on Hitler's first attempt to unite with Austria, turn to page 22 to read about the Dollfuss Affair.

How did Hitler achieve the Anschluss?

In 1934, after Dollfuss' murder, Schuschnigg was appointed Austria's chancellor. He was worried that the Austrian Nazis would attack him, so he made a deal – if they supported him, they would get key jobs in the Austrian government.

↓

By 1938, Austrian Nazis were demonstrating against the government. When police raided their headquarters, they discovered plans to overthrow Schuschnigg.

↓

Schuschnigg panicked and went to meet Hitler. The meeting took place at Hitler's mountain retreat and three Nazi generals were invited, to intimidate Schuschnigg. Hitler demanded that Nazis were given control of the Austrian police, finance and military, that the restrictions on the Nazi Party were lifted and that any Nazis in prison were released. Schuschnigg was given three days to agree, or Hitler would invade.

↓

Schuschnigg agreed, but he decided to hold a plebiscite (a referendum) on the Anschluss. If the people voted against Anschluss, Hitler would not be able to justify an invasion.

↓

In March 1938, Hitler demanded that the plebiscite was delayed. Schuschnigg agreed, because he feared that he would get no support from Britain and France against Hitler. Hitler forced Schuschnigg to resign and made sure a Nazi, Seyss-Inquart, became chancellor.

↓

Seyss-Inquart immediately claimed that Austria was in chaos and asked Hitler for help to restore peace. The next day, 12 March, Nazi troops invaded Austria.

↓

In April 1938, Hitler held a plebiscite. Although it was presented as a free vote, there was heavy pressure to vote in favour of the Anschluss, including the presence of Nazi stormtroopers at polling stations. Ninety-nine per cent of Austrians voted in favour of Anschluss, a major exaggeration of the policy's popularity.

A voting card from the plebiscite in 1938. The question asks people if they are in favour of Anschluss and having Hitler as Führer. The pressure being applied to the Austrian people is shown by the design of the paper: the big circle in the middle is for 'yes', the small one to the side for 'no'.

Austria and Germany – the Anschluss was widely supported in both countries (though pressure played a large part in Austria).

France – although the further weakening of the Treaty of Versailles was a concern, France had bigger problems. The whole French government had resigned after there had been rioting about the economy.

Reactions to Anschluss

Czechoslovakia – the Czechs were very concerned. They knew about Hitler's policy of Lebensraum and worried that they would be next.

Britain – most people in Britain did not object to the Anschluss, seeing Austria and Germany as the same country anyway. Some people, such as Churchill, felt that if Hitler wanted Anschluss he should have negotiated it rather than invading, but they were not opposed to it in principle.

Now try this

Give **three** ways in which the Anschluss made Nazi Germany stronger.

The Sudeten Crisis

By March 1938, Hitler had broken several terms of the Treaty of Versailles, with no response from the major powers (Britain, France, the USA) or the League of Nations. Hitler decided to go even further.

Why did Hitler invade the Sudetenland?

Germany and the Sudetenland, 1938.

Germany surrounded the Sudetenland (formerly part of German Bavaria) on three sides. It would make **a good base for a later attack** on the rest of Czechoslovakia.

About three million **German-speakers** lived in the Sudetenland. Hitler claimed that they were being persecuted.

Czechoslovakia had been formed by the **Treaty of Versailles,** which Hitler wanted to overturn.

Czechoslovakia had a **large army, strong fortifications and industries** that would help Hitler's war effort.

☐ German territory
☐ Sudetenland

Chamberlain and appeasement

The Nazis used the same tactics they'd used in Austria – encouraging demonstrations to weaken the government. In May 1938, Hitler claimed that ethnic Germans were being persecuted and needed protection.

⬇

Britain and France knew that if Hitler invaded Czechoslovakia, they would be obliged to declare war to protect it. They had seen the devastating impact of Germany's Luftwaffe in Spain and decided to do whatever they could to stop Hitler invading.

⬇

Neville Chamberlain, the British prime minister, met Hitler on 15 September 1938. Hitler said that the only way to resolve the crisis was to let him take the Sudetenland. Chamberlain, desperate to avoid war, agreed – as long as the takeover was peaceful.

⬇

However, a week later, on 22 September, Hitler changed his demands. He now wanted the Sudetenland sooner, and for Hungary and Poland to be given land in Czechoslovakia. This was more than Chamberlain had agreed.

For more on appeasement, turn to pages 21, 28 and 29.

Consequences

* The German army marched into the Sudetenland on 1 October 1938.
* This area contained lots of Czechoslovakia's mountain-based militarily defensive positions. Without them, it was completely defenceless against a German invasion of the rest of Czechoslovakia.
* Hitler's success in the Sudetenland made him even bolder and increased his popularity in Germany.

Chamberlain and Hitler greet one another at Munich in 1938.

Now try this

Why did Neville Chamberlain agree to Hitler's demands to take over the Sudetenland? Explain your answer in a short paragraph.

The Munich Conference

Chamberlain's negotiations with Hitler did not seem to be reaching a fixed agreement and war was looking more likely. Mussolini suggested that Germany, Britain, France and Italy should meet to agree Czechoslovakia's borders. The meeting took place in Munich on 29 September 1938 and the Anglo-German declaration was signed the following day.

Hitler's demands

In Munich, Hitler repeated the demands he had made when he met Chamberlain on 22 September:

- Czechoslovakia was to remove its troops from the Sudetenland and allow Germany to take it on Hitler's earlier timetable.
- Hungary and Poland had made claims to Czechoslovakian land and Hitler insisted that these claims were agreed to.

In return, Hitler promised peace in Europe.

Chamberlain and Daladier (the French prime minister) agreed to Hitler's demands. They claimed that by getting Hitler to agree to respect the Czech border and promise peace, they had fulfilled their duty to protect Czechoslovakia from Germany.

The negotiations

Hitler counted on Britain and France being willing to accept his demands to take the Sudetenland in order to avoid war. He was right in his calculation. The USSR would have been prepared to intervene on behalf of Czechoslovakia, but Britain wanted to avoid allying with communists and preferred to allow Hitler to have his way.

Edvard Beneš, Czechoslovakia's leader, was unhappy about the Munich Agreement. He was not involved in the discussions and was simply told by Britain and France that they would not go to war to protect the Sudetenland. Czechoslovakia could either resist Nazi Germany alone or agree to the annexation. The Czechoslovak government knew they could not fight the Nazis alone, so reluctantly gave in and agreed to stick to the agreement.

The Munich Agreement

- Signed 30 September 1938.
- Agreement reached by Germany, Britain, France and Italy.
- Granted Germany the Sudetenland, a region of Czechoslovakia on the German border.
- Three million people in the Sudeten region had German origins.
- Hitler promised that this would be the final expansion of Germany.

It soon became clear that Hitler was intending to expand further, but the Munich Agreement did ensure that the Allies had more time to prepare their military for war.

On 30 September 1938, the British prime minister, Neville Chamberlain, returned to Britain holding the Munich Agreement, and declared that it represented 'peace in our time'.

The Czechoslovak government was not invited to the Munich Conference, or consulted about the Agreement, so it considered the Agreement to be a betrayal by Britain and France. They called the Munich Agreement the 'Munich dliktat' because it was 'about us, but without us'.

Other reactions

German Sudetens were pleased by the Munich Agreement, but the Czechoslovakians felt that it was the start of a full invasion.

The USSR had also not been consulted. Stalin was furious. Britain and France had been trying to get him to promise Soviet support if there was a war, and he felt betrayed. He was also worried that Hitler was becoming more of a threat to the USSR's allies in Eastern Europe.

Now try this

Name **two** problems caused by the Munich Agreement.

Appeasement 1

Hitler had always said that he wanted to overturn the Treaty of Versailles in order to restore German strength. As soon as he took power, he started to do this and war became more likely. Why didn't Britain do more to stop him?

What was appeasement?

Appeasement was an approach used by Britain during the 1930s. Many British people thought that the losing countries, including Germany, had been too harshly punished after the First World War and that what Hitler was asking for was reasonable – so if he was given what he was entitled to, he would be happy and another war would be avoided.

Chamberlain and Hitler at a meeting in Berchtesgaden in 1938. Chamberlain, desperate to avoid war, agreed to let Hitler take the Sudetenland.

Nowadays 'appeasement' has come to mean allowing a bully to get away with their bad behaviour, but in the 1930s many people saw it as a very rational approach to trying to secure peace.

Many people felt that the Treaty of Versailles had been unfair and that Germany's demands were reasonable.

The loss and destruction of the First World War was still fresh in people's minds. Most people had lost loved ones and didn't want to lose more. Peace was supported by the majority.

Knowing that everything possible had been done to avoid war increased British morale when the war began, because they had the moral high ground.

The USA had said they would not get involved in any war in Europe. The lack of such a powerful ally made Britain and France more reluctant to go to war.

Reasons for appeasement

Many of Hitler's actions were backed by the people – for example, the plebiscites in Austria and the Saar overwhelmingly backed Hitler.

More people were worried about the spread of communism than they were about Hitler. A strong Germany would be a buffer between Europe and the USSR.

The Great Depression meant that Britain and France could not afford to fight – they were more interested in solving their own problems.

In the 1930s, Britain was not ready to fight. Rearmament began in 1936, and the government knew it would take several years to be ready for war. Some historians argue that the policy of appeasement was actually just a way of buying time – delaying the war to give them enough time to prepare for it.

Neville Chamberlain, who followed the policy of appeasement, said:

'We should seek by all means in our power to avoid war, by analysing possible causes, by trying to remove them, by discussion in a spirit of collaboration and good will.'

Now try this

In 140 characters or fewer, explain why Britain preferred the policy of appeasement in the 1930s.

Appeasement 2

Appeasement was seen as a reasonable approach to the threat presented by Hitler – but not everyone agreed with it. Some British politicians, like Winston Churchill, were critical of the policy.

The appeasers were wrong to believe Hitler when he said he was only interested in righting the wrongs of Versailles. Hitler had been saying for years that the only way to make Germany strong was to use force. They should have listened.

Czechoslovakia was forced to back down over the Sudetenland, but was a strong country. With a bit of support, Hitler could have been stopped.

For more about the Sudetenland (here in orange), see page 26.

Opportunities to challenge Hitler were missed. For example, if France had challenged the remilitarisation of the Rhineland, Hitler would have had to back down.

Arguments against appeasement

The more Hitler was given, the more he demanded. It should have been clear that appeasement was not going to work.

The Rhineland (here in orange) borders the Alsace-Lorraine region of France. For more about the Rhineland, see page 23.

It was morally wrong to abandon the people of Austria and Czechoslovakia to the Nazis. People suffered as a result of Nazi occupation (especially the Jewish population) and more should have been done to protect them.

It annoyed the USSR. Stalin felt threatened by Hitler but appeasement meant that he didn't think he could rely on support from Britain and France.

'An appeaser is one who feeds a crocodile, hoping it will eat him last.'

Winston Churchill in 1939. Churchill opposed appeasement because he thought Hitler would keep pushing for more.

When you answer questions about the reasons for and against appeasement, remember to think about **hindsight** (understanding of an event that is only possible once it has happened). We know that the policy of appeasement didn't work, but people at the time could not have known for certain. When you make an argument, ask yourself, 'Is this something people at the time would have known?'

Now try this

Which of the arguments against appeasement do you think is strongest? Give **two** reasons for your answer.

Invasion of Czechoslovakia

In March 1939, Hitler invaded Czechoslovakia. It was clear that no amount of appeasement would be sufficient to stop his takeover of further countries in Europe.

Hitler and the expansion of Germany

By 1938, it was clear that Hitler was prepared to use aggression to unite the people of 'Greater Germany' and undo the territorial losses of the Treaty of Versailles.

If Czechoslovakia was annexed by Hitler, Poland was very likely to be next.

German expansion, 1933–1939.

The Sudetenland was annexed by Hitler after the Munich Conference in September 1938.

Hitler invaded the Rhineland, a demilitarised zone, in 1936.

Germany annexed Austria via the Anschluss in 1938.

Once Hitler had taken the Sudetenland, Czechoslovakia was very vulnerable to invasion.

The invasion

| The Munich Agreement left Czechoslovakia weakened, and Hitler became confident that Britain and France were too afraid of war to challenge him. | In March 1939, Hitler summoned the Czechoslovakian president, Emil Hácha, to Berlin and informed him of the imminent invasion. | Hitler persuaded Hácha to order the surrender of the Czechoslovakian army by threatening a Luftwaffe attack on Prague, the capital. | This meant that when German troops marched into Czechoslovakia on 15 March 1939, they met little resistance. |

For more on the Munich Agreement, turn to page 27.

Hitler had occupied a country he had no claim to – there were no German speakers outside the Sudetenland. He could no longer claim to be uniting German people.

Britain and France had to accept that Hitler was not simply reclaiming what had been lost at Versailles.

Chamberlain promised Poland – which seemed likely to be Hitler's next target – that Britain would intervene to protect it.

What was important about the occupation of Czechoslovakia?

Hitler broke the promises he had made in the Munich Agreement. Chamberlain had to accept that the policy of appeasement had failed.

Germany gained about 2000 field cannon, 450 tanks and 40 000 machine guns from its occupation of Czechoslovakia. This was enough weaponry to arm around half of the Wehrmacht.

Page 27 on the Munich Agreement will help you with this question.

Now try this

Write a short paragraph (4–6 lines) explaining why the policy of appeasement finally ended after the occupation of Czechoslovakia.

The Nazi-Soviet Pact

Hitler had been very open about his hatred of communism. Stalin had been suspicious of Hitler for years. In 1939, the two enemies became allies. Why was this?

What was the Nazi-Soviet Pact?

Poland was created at the end of the First World War by taking land from both Russia (later, the USSR) and Germany. Unsurprisingly, both countries were unhappy about this and wanted to reclaim their territory.

After the occupation of Czechoslovakia, Poland was the next target for Hitler's Lebensraum, but he knew that if he invaded, Stalin would intervene. Hitler didn't want to risk this, so he offered Stalin a deal: if the USSR allowed Germany to invade Poland, the USSR would be given some Polish territory. Stalin agreed and a non-aggression pact was signed on 23 August 1939.

What was in it for Germany?

During the First World War, Germany had fought a war on two fronts (there were enemies on two sides of the country).

Germany's troops were divided between the two fronts in the First World War, and this meant a weakened army. Hitler did not want to repeat this mistake. He knew that war with Britain and France was likely, and he wanted to take the USSR – and its huge army – out of the picture. The Nazi-Soviet Pact helped him to ensure this.

The role of the USSR: what was in it for Stalin?

👍 Stalin could reclaim land in Poland, without having to fight for it himself. Hitler would do the fighting for him and hand over the land.

👍 Stalin knew that Hitler would turn on him eventually, but the pact allowed him to buy time to prepare.

Stalin was wise not to trust Hitler – Germany invaded the USSR in 1941.

👍 Reclaiming territory in Poland would help create a 'buffer zone' to protect the USSR if Hitler decided to invade Russia.

👍 Stalin no longer trusted Britain and France. They had not consulted him over the Munich Agreement, and the USSR was isolated. Stalin could not rely on support if Hitler attacked, so he was forced into the pact.

Stalin saw how weak the League of Nations was and had no confidence in the League, or the large powers, to protect him from Hitler.

Stalin was not invited to the Munich Conference or consulted on the Agreement.

Why didn't Stalin trust Britain and France?

The policy of appeasement was justified by the idea that Hitler could provide a barrier between western Europe and communism in the USSR. This made it clear that Britain and France didn't trust Stalin.

Hitler showed Stalin more respect than Chamberlain did, for example by sending more senior diplomats to negotiate with him.

Significance of the Nazi-Soviet Pact

- Hitler now knew that he could invade Poland without facing a war on two fronts.
- After the breakdown of appeasement following the invasion of Czechoslovakia, Britain and France had promised to protect Poland.
- If war broke out, the powerful Soviet army would not side with the Allies.
- The pact made war seem imminent – Britain got ready to fight.

Now try this

Give **two** ways in which the Nazi-Soviet Pact contributed to the outbreak of the Second World War.

Invasion of Poland

By September 1939, Hitler had promises of political support from Mussolini and was ready to invade Poland. The invasion led to the declaration of war within days.

The invasion of Poland and the declaration of war

31 March 1939: Chamberlain promised the Poles that he would protect Poland's borders if Hitler invaded.

⬇

1 September 1939: At dawn, the German navy attacked the port of Danzig.

⬇

1 September: Poland asked for help from France and Britain.

⬇

3 September: Britain and France declared war on Germany.

Danzig was a German port which was made independent in the Treaty of Versailles. It was run by Poland, but about 90% of the population was German.

Meanwhile, ground troops and the German air force launched the invasion of Poland. The whole Polish air force was destroyed on the ground.

Britain and France waited three days before declaring war because they were still hoping Hitler would back down.

Hitler's motives for invading Poland

Hitler was confident about the success of the invasion.

Hitler believed that a war in Poland would be quick and easy.

He was convinced that Neville Chamberlain and Edouard Daladier would continue their policy of appeasement.

The Nazi-Soviet Pact meant that Hitler knew that he would only have to fight on one front, because Stalin would not stop him.

Hitler's previous invasions had been swift and unchallenged, so he thought the invasion of Poland would be the same.

The German army was not completely ready for war and the German economy was not geared up for wartime production. Some of Hitler's generals suggested more time to complete the defences to the west in an attempt to block a future British and French counter-attack. Hitler ignored their suggestion and made them swear oaths of loyalty to him.

Britain declares war

On 3 September 1939, the British ambassador in Berlin delivered a message to the German government. The message said Germany had until 11 am to promise to withdraw from Poland, otherwise Britain would declare war.

No reply came by the deadline. At 11.15 a.m., Chamberlain announced on the radio that Britain was at war with Germany. France declared war shortly afterwards.

Chamberlain announcing on the radio that Britain was at war.

Now try this

In **two** sentences, explain why the invasion of Poland resulted in war when Hitler's previous invasions had not.

Second World War: causes 1

It is easy to argue that the Second World War had one cause: Hitler. But historians think it is much more complicated than that, and that a number of factors played a part in the outbreak of war in 1939.

The Treaty of Versailles, 28 June 1919

1 The treaty was seen by many as too harsh on Germany – the severity of the terms caused great resentment and Hitler was able to turn this to his advantage.

2 Because people had sympathy with Hitler's desire to overturn the treaty, he was allowed to get away with so much that he became confident that nobody would stop him.

3 The creation of Poland by taking land from Germany and the USSR caused resentment and tension – which led to Stalin agreeing to the Nazi-Soviet Pact.

4 The new states created, such as Czechoslovakia and Poland, contained a lot of German people, which Hitler then aimed to reunite.

For more on the Treaty of Versailles, see pages 3–9.

The failure of the League of Nations, 1930–1939

1 The League was weakened from the start by the absence of the USA. Without the USA as a member, the effect of sanctions was reduced, meaning the League could not take effective action. This encouraged dictators like Hitler and Mussolini.

2 Because key powers were not members (USA, Germany, Russia), important diplomacy took place outside the League, which weakened its position. The Hoare-Laval Pact showed that Britain and France would undermine the League if it suited them, which made it useless as a peacekeeping organisation.

3 The failure to act in Manchuria showed that the League was not strong enough to stand up to countries that broke the rules.

4 The Abyssinian Crisis showed that the lack of an army stopped the League taking effective action, even against a country that was clearly in the wrong.

For more on the League of Nations, see pages 10–15.

The Great Depression, 1929–1939

1 The Great Depression increased the USA's determination to pursue a policy of isolationism, which weakened international cooperation.

2 The extreme poverty and high unemployment meant that dictators like Mussolini and Hitler began to appeal to people by giving them someone to blame and promising to put things right.

3 The Great Depression caused economic and social problems all over the world. Governments were more interested in solving their own problems than getting involved in international politics.

4 The League of Nations could not impose effective sanctions because member countries were reluctant to damage trade.

5 The Great Depression meant that nobody could afford to take part in military action that wasn't absolutely necessary.

For more on the Great Depression, see page 16.

For example, you might write: 'The Great Depression contributed to the failure of the League of Nations because it made countries reluctant to impose sanctions.'

Now try this

Look at the factors on this page: the Treaty of Versailles, the failure of the League of Nations and the Great Depression. Find **two** links between these factors.

Second World War: causes 2

As well as understanding how events contributed to the outset of war, you need to consider the roles played by key individuals.

Chamberlain and appeasement

For more on appeasement, see pages 26–29.

1 In the late 1930s, people all over Europe were desperate to avoid another war – the impact of the First World War had been horrendous. The majority of people in Britain supported appeasement.

2 Opportunities to stop Hitler were missed, such as the remilitarisation of the Rhineland. If he had been challenged then, he would have had to back down.

3 Some historians argue that Chamberlain should not have trusted Hitler – especially because Hitler had made no secret of his plans since the 1920s.

4 Appeasement was partly motivated by a fear of communism, which meant Stalin gradually lost faith in the Allies.

5 The Munich Agreement was the final straw for Stalin, and this led to the Nazi-Soviet Pact.

Hitler and his aggressive foreign policies

1 Hitler was aggressive from the start. In his book *Mein Kampf*, he said that the only way to regain Germany's strength was through violence, by overturning the Treaty of Versailles, uniting German-speaking people and taking Lebensraum.

For more on Hitler's foreign policy, see pages 20–26.

2 Hitler hated communism and wanted to destroy it. To do this, he would have to attack the USSR.

3 Achieving Hitler's policy of Lebensraum was only possible by invading other countries. There was nothing other than war that would stop him.

Stalin and the Nazi-Soviet Pact

For more on the Nazi-Soviet Pact, see page 31.

1 The pact with Stalin meant that Hitler did not have to worry about a war on two fronts – knowing he could concentrate on the west made him confident.

2 Although Stalin was not going to get directly involved to support Hitler, he was not going to support the Allies either.

3 The pact made the invasion of Poland inevitable – and, as Britain and France had promised to support Poland, it led directly to the outbreak of war.

Causation

Causation is the word historians use to describe finding out **why** something happened. Understanding causation is a vital historical skill.

It's rare that any event has just one single cause. Causation can be divided into three periods:

☑ long-term causes
☑ short-term causes
☑ triggers.

Long-term causes are things that happened many years before the event.
Short-term causes are things that happened more recently.
A **trigger** is the final straw – the event that finally causes something else to happen. It might not be the most important cause.

Now try this

Re-read the information on this page and on page 33. Then list **three** long-term causes, **two** short-term causes and **one** trigger for the Second World War.

Exam overview

This page introduces you to the main features and requirements of the Paper 1 Section B exam paper for Conflict and tension, 1918–1939.

About Paper 1

- Paper 1 is for your period study and your wider world depth study.

- Section B of the paper will be on your wider world depth study, which is Conflict and tension, 1918–1939.

- Section B will include questions about other wider world depth study options. You should **only** answer the questions about Conflict and tension, 1918–1939.

- You will receive two documents: a question paper, which will contain the questions and sources, and an answer booklet.

The Paper 1 exam lasts for 1 hour 45 minutes (105 minutes). There are 84 marks in total: 40 marks for Section A; **40 marks for Section B, plus 4 marks for spelling, punctuation and grammar.** You should spend about 50 minutes on Section A and **50 minutes on Section B**, with 5 minutes to check your answers.

Here we are focusing on Section B and your wider world depth study. However, the same exam paper will also include Section A, where you will answer questions on your period study.

The questions

The questions for Paper 1 Section B will always follow this pattern:

You can see examples of all four questions on pages 39–44, and in the practice questions on pages 45–54.

Question 11

Study **Source D**.

Source D … How do you know?

Explain your answer using **Source D** and your contextual knowledge.   **(4 marks)**

Question 11 targets AO3. AO3 is about analysing, evaluating and using sources to make substantiated judgements. Spend about 6 minutes on this question, which focuses on **analysing a source** and using your own **contextual knowledge**.

Question 12

Study **Sources E** and **F**.

How useful are **Sources E** and **F** to a historian studying …?

Explain your answer using **Sources E** and **F** and your contextual knowledge.   **(12 marks)**

Question 12 also targets AO3. Spend about 14 minutes on this question, which is about **evaluating sources** and using your own **contextual knowledge**.

Question 13

Write an account …   **(8 marks)**

Question 13 targets AO1 and AO2. AO1 is about showing your knowledge and understanding of the key features and characteristics of the topic. AO2 is about explaining and analysing historical events using second order concepts such as causation, consequence, change, continuity, similarity and difference. Spend about 10 minutes on this question, which requires you to write a **narrative account**.

Question 14

[Statement]

How far do you agree with this statement?

Explain your answer.

                (16 marks, plus 4 marks for SPaG)

Question 14 also targets AO1 and AO2. Spend about 20 minutes on this question, which requires you to make a **judgement** in an **extended response**. Up to 4 marks are available for **spelling, punctuation and grammar** (SPaG).

Source skills

Questions 11 and 12 are based on **sources**. Question 11 asks you to **analyse one source**, and Question 12 asks you to **evaluate the usefulness of two different sources**.

What is a source?

A source is something that comes from the time period or event it describes.

A source can be text, such as:

- an account written by someone at the time, such as a letter or diary
- a speech
- a book or government report
- a poem or work of fiction
- a newspaper or magazine article.

It might also be visual, such as:

- a cartoon, photograph, poster or painting
- a plan of a building
- an advertisement
- an object such as a coin or postcard.

Contextual knowledge

✓ Questions 11 and 12 will both ask you to explain your answer using the sources and your **contextual knowledge**.

✓ This means that you need to think about what you know about the event or development and how the sources fit with what you know.

✓ Only use knowledge that is **relevant** to the topic in the question and that is linked to what is contained in the source itself.

Analysing sources

Analysing the source means working out what it's saying. For example, Question 11 asks you to look at a source and use your contextual knowledge to explain how it conveys a particular idea. To do this, think about:

- What is the **intended message** (purpose) of the source?
- What else can we **infer** (work out) from it? Remember, this may not be something the person who created the source intended!
- What can we tell from the **provenance** (origin and nature) of the source?
- Does the information in the source agree with your **contextual knowledge**? What does this tell you?

Evaluating sources

To evaluate the **usefulness** of a source, you need to look at the content, provenance and the context as well as the source itself. For example, Question 12 asks you to evaluate the usefulness of two sources.

1 **Content**
- What information in the sources is relevant to the enquiry?
- How useful is this information?

 Underline and annotate information in the source to help you with this.

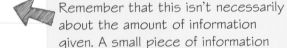 Remember that this isn't necessarily about the amount of information given. A small piece of information can be very useful!

2 **Provenance**
- Nature: the type of source it is.
- Origins: who produced it and when.
- Purpose: the reason the source was created.
- How do these things impact on the usefulness of the source?

Remember that an unreliable source can still be useful.

3 **Context**
- Use your own knowledge of the enquiry topic to evaluate the source.
- Is the information in the source accurate compared with what you know?

 Remember to think about what information is missing from the source as well as what's included.

Source D

This source is referred to in the worked example on page 39.

SECTION B

Conflict and tension, 1918–1939

Source D   A poster produced in Germany in 1932. The words in German mean 'Versailles. War Guilt Lies 231'.

You will be given short details on where the source comes from – in this case, the type of source and where and when it was produced.

You will be given some information about the source. In this case, you are told that the source is about the Treaty of Versailles.

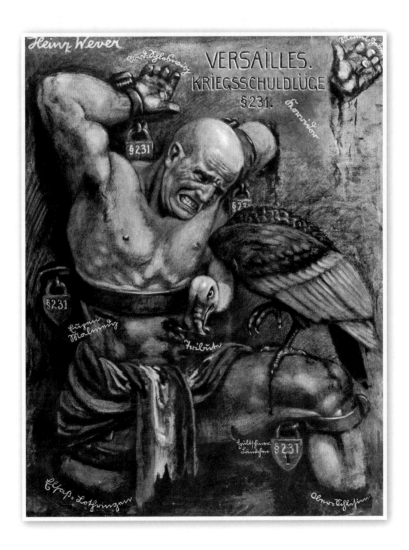

Sources E and F

These sources are referred to in the worked examples on pages 40–41.

Source E   A German cartoon from 1925 showing (left–right) French statesman Aristide Briand, British foreign minister Austen Chamberlain and German foreign minister Gustave Stresemann at the Locarno Conference. Germany (represented by Stresemann) is shown in debtors' chains.

Annotate the sources with your ideas. If the source is an image, like this one, think about the details you can see and what they might mean.

Source F   From a speech made by Gustav Stresemann after the negotiation of the Locarno treaties, 16 October 1925.

> The Treaty of Locarno ... is destined to be a landmark in the history of the relations of States and peoples to each other. We especially welcome the expressed conviction set forth in this final protocol that our labours will lead to decreased tension among the peoples and to an easier solution of so many political and economic problems ... Locarno is not to be the end but the beginning of confident cooperation among the nations. That these prospects, and the hopes based upon our work, may come to fruition is the earnest wish to which the German delegates would give expression at this solemn moment.

If the source is a text extract, underline or highlight any important words or phrases and annotate them.

Question 11: analysing sources

Question 11 on your exam paper will ask you to explain 'How you know ....' something about a source, using the source and your own knowledge of the **historical context**. There are 4 marks available for this question.

Worked example

Study **Source D** on page 37.

Source D is critical of the Treaty of Versailles. How do you know?

Explain your answer using **Source D** and your contextual knowledge.   **(4 marks)**

 Links You can revise attitudes to the Treaty of Versailles on pages 5–6.

Analysing a source

Analysing a source is working out what it means, including meanings that aren't directly shown.

✓ Think about what is suggested or implied by the source.

✓ Look at the **context** and **provenance** of the source too.

You need to **explain** how the source supports the statement in the question by:

✓ referring to details in the source and linking them to your contextual knowledge.

For more on analysing sources, turn to page 36.

Sample answer

I know the poster is critical of the Treaty of Versailles. The man in the poster looks like he is angry. He is wearing chains on his arms and legs. He is trying to get away but he can't. I think the chains are supposed to be the Treaty of Versailles because the people in Germany thought that it was a bad treaty and they wanted to get out of it but they couldn't.

The student describes the picture and highlights some relevant information but they only give limited analysis of the message of the poster.

The student needs to use contextual knowledge to explain what the details in the source are referring to.

Improved answer

I know that the poster is critical of the Versailles treaty because of the imagery used in the poster. It shows a strong man, representing the people of Germany, who has been put in shackles by those who imposed the Versailles treaty, the Allies, in particular Britain and France. The source represents how the terms of the treaty made the German people suffer and held them back from recovering after the war. The numbers 231 are shown on the image. This was the 'war guilt' clause of the treaty that said that Germany was guilty for starting the war and it had to pay reparations for the damage caused to the Allies. France was very keen to force the reparations payments as so much fighting, and therefore damage, had been done on French soil. This aspect of the treaty was the most hated and resented by the German public, and far right extremists like Hitler seized on this resentment in building support for his nationalist ideas. They said the treaty was a 'shameful diktat' imposed on Germany and should be ended for the sake of Germany.

 Consider the intended **audience, message** and **the reason** the source was produced (its purpose). Also think about **when** it was produced as this context will help you to **analyse** the source, rather than just describe it.

Think about what you can see and then move on to think about what it **suggests**. Don't just describe the source – you need to go further and show you understand what the author or artist is trying to say.

 This answer includes relevant and detailed knowledge of the **historical context** of the source, in this case the attitudes of the German people towards the Treaty of Versailles.

Question 12: evaluating usefulness 1

Question 12 on your exam paper will ask you to evaluate the usefulness of two sources. There are 12 marks available for this question.

Worked example

Study Sources E and F on page 38.

How useful are **Sources E** and **F** to a historian studying the Locarno treaties of 1925?

Explain your answer using **Sources E** and **F** and your contextual knowledge.

(12 marks)

 Links Turn to page 15 to revise the Locarno treaties.

Compare this answer with an improved version on the next page.

Evaluating the usefulness of sources

To judge the usefulness of a source, you need to think about the content of the source, and its provenance.

To evaluate the **content**, look carefully at the source and what it shows. How would it help someone understand the topic mentioned in the question? What details are included? Compare these details with your historical knowledge. Is there anything you would expect to see that isn't there?

To judge the **provenance**, think about what the source is, where it came from and what it was intended for (its purpose).

You have two sources to consider, so evaluate the pros and cons of each. Do the sources complement each other? (This means that using both together gives you a fuller picture.)

For more on evaluating sources, turn to page 36.

Sample answer

Sources E and F are both about the Locarno treaties of 1925. In source E, the German politician Stresemann is shown wearing chains that are weighing him down. The other people in the picture are politicians who are treating him badly and have all the power. Stresemann does not look happy about the arrangement but he looks trapped like he has no choice about what the others are doing.

In Source F, Stresemann makes a speech at the conference. He is very positive about the event and says Locarno 'will lead to decreased tension'. He wants people hearing the speech to think that the agreement is good for Germany and good for the future.

Source E is negative about Locarno and portrays Germany as powerless, which shows that some people in Germany were angry about the treaties. However, Source F is very positive about them. Stresemann wants people to think that he has done the right thing. It's useful for finding out about this topic because Stresemann actually made the agreements himself and this is what he thought about them.

Be careful not to just describe what you can see in the source. This part of the answer identifies some good details, but the student needs to analyse what these details tell us and think about **how useful** the source is to a historian studying the treaties.

The student begins to **evaluate** the source by thinking about the speaker and what he was trying to do when he made this speech. However, the student does not fully explain the question of usefulness by discussing what it tells us about the Locarno treaties.

 The student begins to **evaluate** the sources' usefulness, but this part of the answer needs to be developed further.

Question 12: evaluating usefulness 2

This page has an improved version of the answer given on page 40.

Improved answer

Both sources E and F are useful for a historian studying the Locarno treaties. Source E is a German cartoon produced in 1932 about the Locarno Conference. As such, it shows that some people in Germany were highly critical of the agreements which they believed were damaging Germany as a nation.

It depicts Stresemann as a debtor in chains, while other politicians look on to see the consequences for Germany and those who have treated them so badly. German nationalists believed that the Locarno Pact was not good for Germany because it was another example of Germany accepting the terms first agreed in the Treaty of Versailles. For example, Germany agreed to accept its new western borders and all the countries involved agreed to avoid military force except in self-defence. Germany also agreed that Alsace-Lorraine would be French and France agreed not to occupy the Ruhr again. The source is useful because it shows that some sections of public opinion in Germany were negative despite the fact that Stresemann was awarded the Nobel Peace Prize in 1926 for his achievements in improving foreign relations. On its own, the cartoon has limited use because it does not tell us the extent of criticism of the Locarno treaties.

Source F is useful as it gives us an insight into how Stresemann presented the Locarno Pact to the public. He presents the agreement in a very positive way, calling it a historical 'landmark'. However, as a speech it shows want he wanted the public to think about the Locarno Pact rather than the full picture of how effective it was for advancing foreign relations at that time.

Stresemann was always keen to work with other nations to improve their relationships. In this way, he hoped that the terms agreed might be reviewed in time and less harsh penalties secured, thereby helping the German nation to fully recover from the impact of the war. In his speech, he says he hopes that the Locarno Pact would lead to reduced 'tension among the peoples and to an easier solution'. It is very useful for providing an insight into Stresemann's motives, whereas source E is more useful for estimating public reactions.

Start with a clear **introductory statement** that links directly to the question. Here, the student then goes on to look at the **provenance** of the first source and consider what that tells us.

Contextual knowledge

Don't forget that this question also requires you to include your contextual knowledge. You need to show that you understand what was going on at the time the sources were created and how this might impact on their usefulness. For example, did the creator of the source have all the information, or were they biased? Your contextual knowledge must be directly relevant to this question.

Relate the details in the source to your own **contextual knowledge**. Here, the student links the depiction of Stresemann in the cartoon with the views of nationalists in Germany.

Make sure that you evaluate the source by considering its **content** and **purpose** – here the student explains the impact the source would have on its audience.

Focus on evaluating and making judgements about the **usefulness** of the sources, not just describing them. Make sure you keep relating the source to your contextual knowledge.

This answer uses specific language, such as: 'insight', 'depict', 'effective', 'presents'. Using specific language makes your argument clearer and your answer more focused.

Question 13: narrative account

Question 13 on your exam paper requires you to write a narrative account analysing how and why a historical event happened. There are 8 marks available for this question.

Worked example

Write an account of how the Abyssinian Crisis weakened the League of Nations in 1936.

(8 marks)

🔗 Links You can revise the Abyssinian Crisis on page 18.

What is a narrative account?

A **narrative account** is not simply a description of what happened. To write a successful narrative account, you need to:

- ✓ think about **key elements** of the event and how they were **connected**
- ✓ consider what you have been asked to do – you may need to think about **cause**, **change**, **continuity** and/or **consequence** here
- ✓ use your **own knowledge** of the period
- ✓ structure your narrative logically, so it clearly explains the **sequence** of events.

Sample extract

Mussolini's invasion of Abyssinia in 1935 led to a significantly weakened League of Nations by 1936. International tensions in the 1930s were running high. Mussolini was keen to encourage Italian nationalism and empire building was key to this ambition. In 1928, Mussolini signed a peace treaty with Haile Selassie, the emperor of Abyssinia, but he was already planning his invasion.

When Abyssinia appealed to the League of Nations, the League announced economic sanctions against Italy to pressurise Mussolini to withdraw. However, the agreement on sanctions took six weeks and did not include essentials like bans on trading oil, coal and steel. This was because the League thought that it was pointless as Italy could still trade with non-League members like the USA. This showed an important weakness in the League's ability to impose effective sanctions. To make matters worse, some League members did not stick to the sanctions. Other actions, like shutting the Suez Canal, would have stopped Italy sending supplies and weapons to Abyssinia, but this was not done because Britain and France wanted to keep Mussolini as an ally against Hitler.

The League of Nations was weakened because key members showed that they were interested in world affairs only when it had a direct impact on them (for example, the Hoare-Laval Pact). Worse than this, it became clear that the League was unable to make members keep to the covenant, and there was no consequence for breaking it – this showed dictators like Hitler and Mussolini that the League would not oppose them.

Start with a **clear introduction** which relates to the question and signposts your argument. This need only be a sentence or two.

Use your **own knowledge** of the period. Here, the information about Mussolini's ambitions shows the use of relevant knowledge.

🔗 Links You can revise the role of Mussolini on pages 18, 19 and 24.

The student presents a clear account of how one thing led to another by linking the event – in this case, the disagreement over sanctions – to the result – in this case, the fact that it showed that the League was weak and unable to impose consequences.

Your answer should relate to the question being asked. Here, the student gives a clear and detailed explanation of the effect of the Abyssinian Crisis on the League of Nations.

Explain clearly how the events led to the consequence. Here, the student has not only recounted the key events in **sequence** but explained how they were connected, why they were important and how they led to the weakening of the League.

Question 14: extended response 1

Question 14 on your exam paper will ask you to write an **extended response** showing a sustained line of reasoning and making a judgement. You will be given a statement and asked **how far** you agree with it. There are 16 marks available for this question, plus four marks for spelling, punctuation, grammar and use of historical terminology.

Worked example

'The main reason why Germany signed the armistice was its unstable domestic situation.'

How far do you agree with this statement?

Explain your answer.

(16 marks, plus 4 marks for SPaG)

🔗 **Links**   You can revise the armistice on page 1.

It can be helpful to write a list of points **for** and **against** the judgement in the question before you start writing your answer.

'How far…' questions

This question asks you to weigh **evidence** to come up with an argument – a **line of reasoning**. You need to:

- ☑ describe any evidence that supports the statement in the question, explaining why it **supports** the statement
- ☑ do the same for any evidence that **contradicts** the statement
- ☑ develop a **sustained** line of reasoning – 'sustained' means you need to present a clear, logical argument **throughout your answer**
- ☑ make a **judgement** – you need to decide 'how far' you agree by reaching a conclusion based on the evidence and reasoning in your answer.

Sample answer

I don't agree with the statement that the main reason Germany agreed to the armistice was what was going on in Germany.

On the front line, the Germans were struggling to make progress. After America had joined the Allies in 1917, it was obvious that Germany was going to struggle to match the manpower and resources of their opponents. The military situation for Germany was getting worse.

The politicians who agreed to the armistice did not want to sign it. When they met in a remote railway carriage in the Forest of Compiègne, north of Paris, the terms were designed to make it impossible for Germany to start fighting the war again. It was forced to hand over its heavy guns and its field guns, as well as another 25 000 machine guns, its aircraft and all its submarines. It also had to give up its warships. This would have been difficult to do, but Germany had no real choice as it could not continue to fight without risking an invasion by the Allies.

That is why I believe that the main reason for Germany agreeing to the armistice was not the domestic situation.

Compare this answer with an improved version on the next page.

 Start your answer with a clear statement, signposting your argument.

 All your points should be supported with **evidence**. Here, the student gives basic evidence but this could be expanded.

 Remember that you should only include information that is **relevant** to the question. This answer contains facts that are not directly relevant to evaluating the judgement in the question. Rather than describing the armistice, the answer should examine **why** the Germans agreed to it.

Make sure that you **examine both sides** of the argument. Here, the student develops a line of argument but it is limited to Germany's military issues, and does not discuss the issue mentioned in the question.

Question 14: extended response 2

This page has an improved version of the answer on page 43.

Improved answer

I agree that the domestic situation in Germany was significant in explaining its decision to sign the armistice. However, it is not the main reason.

Germany's domestic situation was very unstable. In Berlin, crowds of civilians protested on the streets. The population was exhausted by the war effort. The strain of mass food shortages was made worse by extreme rationing, leading to famine in some areas. The Spanish flu outbreak killed thousands and lowered morale even further. The economy collapsed and led Germany to the brink of civil war. The chancellor, Prince Max, believed that the only way to resolve the social unrest was to declare a German republic led by the socialists, so on 9 November 1918 he announced the creation of a new German republic. The kaiser escaped to Holland where he stayed in exile to avoid the possibility of a civil war. It was clear that Germany could not continue like this for long.

However, even more important in explaining the decision to sign the armistice were the military problems that the Germans were experiencing. Soldiers in the trenches did not know the reality of the situation as their officers were determined to maintain the lie that victory was almost theirs. However, those in charge knew that Germany was short of soldiers and supplies and would soon have enemy troops invading their country. The entry of the USA into the war meant that the Allies had far greater numbers of soldiers and resources. In the German port of Kiel, sailors had mutinied and refused to fight the British, certain that they would be killed. It was becoming very clear that Germany could not win the war – agreeing to an armistice was the only way to avoid even more damage and loss of life.

In conclusion, I would argue that although the domestic situation was an important factor, the German military situation was more important in explaining why they agreed to the armistice. If they had been able to win, they would have continued the conflict for longer.

This introduction clearly signposts that the answer will consider **both sides** of the argument.

Highlighting key points raised by the statement will help you focus on the arguments that you need to **evaluate** to make your judgement.

This paragraph explores the problems of Germany's domestic situation and the impact that had on the decision to end the war.

Starting a paragraph with words and phrases such as 'However' or 'On the other hand' clearly demonstrates that you are moving on to another part of your argument, and shows that your answer is following a clear **structure** and has a **sustained line of reasoning**.

Remember that, for this question, 4 additional marks are available for good **spelling**, **grammar**, **punctuation** and use of historical **terminology**.

Use **specific historical vocabulary**, such as 'armistice', 'military', 'defeat', 'civilian', 'domestic' to make sure your answer is really focused.

Finish with a clear **conclusion**, summarising the main arguments and stating clearly 'how far' you agree with the statement.

Practice

You will need to refer to the source below in your answer to question 11 on page 47.

SECTION B

Conflict and tension, 1918–1939

Source D   A German postcard from 1938. The words in German say '13 March 1938, One people, One empire, One leader'.

13·MÄRZ 1938
EIN VOLK EIN REICH
EIN FÜHRER

Practice

You will need to refer to the sources below in your answer to question 12 on page 48.

Source E   A British cartoon published in 'Punch' magazine on 26 March 1919.

OVERWEIGHTED.

PRESIDENT WILSON. "HERE'S YOUR OLIVE BRANCH. NOW GET BUSY."
DOVE OF PEACE. "OF COURSE I WANT TO PLEASE EVERYBODY; BUT ISN'T THIS A
BIT THICK?"

Source F   From a speech by US president, Woodrow Wilson, on the League of Nations,
8 September 1919.

Only two nations are for the time being left out. One of them is Germany,
because we did not think that Germany was ready to come in, because we felt
that she ought to go through a period of probation. She says that she made a
mistake. We now want her to prove it by not trying it again. She says that she
has abolished all the old forms of government by which little secret councils of
men, sitting nobody knew exactly where, determined the fortunes of that great
nation and, incidentally, tried to determine the fortunes of mankind; but we want
her to prove that her constitution is changed and that it is going to stay changed;
and then who can, after those proofs are produced, say 'No' to a great people,
60 million strong, if they want to come in on equal terms with the rest of us and
do justice in international affairs?

Practice

Put your skills and knowledge into practice with the following question. You will need to refer to Source D on page 45 in your answer.

11 Study **Source D**.

Source D is a postcard in support of Hitler's foreign policy. How do you know?

Explain your answer using **Source D** and your contextual knowledge.

(4 marks)

Guided   The postcard shows a map of the 'Greater Germany' with Hitler's head positioned prominently in the centre. The message is

....

....

....

....

....

....

....

....

....

....

....

....

....

....

....

....

You have 1 hour 45 minutes for the **whole** of Paper 1, which means you have 50 minutes for Section B. You should use the time carefully to answer all the questions fully. In the exam, remember to leave 5 minutes or so to check your work when you've finished both Sections A and B.

Spend about 6 minutes on this answer. You need to identify features in the source and use your own knowledge.

Links. You can revise Hitler's foreign policy tactics on pages 20 and 22–27.

You can revise how to analyse sources on page 36.

Remember to make **inferences** from the source to show you are analysing it. This means working something out that isn't shown directly.

An example of a suitable inference might be that 'The Nazis were keen to convey their message about empire building. They were determined to make Hitler look all-powerful and unstoppable.'

Make a claim based on evidence you take from the source (in this case the postcard) about the intended **purpose** of the source: who its message was aimed at and why.

Make sure you give **examples** of details from the source to back up what you say.

Link your argument to your **contextual knowledge** of the period.

Practice

Put your skills and knowledge into practice with the following question. You will need to refer to Sources E and F on page 46 in your answer.

12 Study **Sources E** and **F**.

How useful are **Sources E** and **F** to a historian studying the formation of the League of Nations?

Explain your answer, using **Sources E** and **F** and your contextual knowledge.

(12 marks)

Guided Both Sources E and F are useful for finding out

about the formation of the League of Nations because

....

....

....

....

....

....

....

....

....

....

....

....

....

....

....

....

....

....

....

....

....

You should spend about 14 minutes on this answer.

'Useful' means you have to judge what the source tells you about the question you are being asked. You will also need to think about what the problems with the source could be.

Links You can revise the League of Nations on pages 10–14.

You can revise how to evaluate sources on page 36.

Remember, you need to identify and **evaluate** the pros and cons of **both** sources and make a judgement.

Make sure you include some examples from your **contextual knowledge**. Don't just rely on the content and provenance of the sources.

Practice

Use this page to continue your answer to question 12.

....
....
....
....
....
....
....
....
....
....
....
....
....
....
....
....
....
....
....
....
....
....
....
....
....

Think: Are there any aspects of the sources that make them less **useful**? You might find it helpful to consider the **provenance** of the two sources here.

Practice

Put your skills and knowledge into practice with the following question.

13 Write an account of how the economic depression after 1929 led to problems for the League of Nations.

(8 marks)

Guided Economic conditions after 1929 led to a range of problems for the League of Nations and contributed to its collapse.

....

....

....

....

....

....

....

....

....

....

....

....

....

....

....

....

....

....

....

....

....

You should spend about 10 minutes on this question.

'Write an account' means you have to give a narrative that **explains the connections**, and does not just describe what happened.

Links You can revise the economic depression on page 16.

Keep your answer focused on the question. You might remember lots of detail about the Depression, but you need to focus on the problems it caused for the League of Nations.

Make sure you use your **own knowledge** of the period to describe how factors combined to bring about an outcome — in this case, how different factors came together that resulted in the problems of the League of Nations.

Make sure your answer **analyses the links** between factors. Try to use phrases such as: 'this was because', 'this led to', 'the result of this was ...', 'the factors that caused this were ...'. This will help you make sure that your answer follows a **logical structure**.

Practice

Use this page to continue your answer to question 13.

....
....
....
....
....
....
....
....
....
....
....
....
....

Finish with a clear **conclusion** to summarise your account.

Practice

Put your skills and knowledge into practice with the following question.

14 'The main reason why Germany hated the Treaty of Versailles was because of Article 231, the war guilt clause.' How far do you agree with this statement? Explain your answer.

(16 marks, plus 4 marks for SPaG)

Guided The Treaty of Versailles was widely resented in Germany for a range of reasons. The war guilt clause was particularly hated, but it was not the only aspect that led to the German public's resentment of the peace settlement.

....

....

....

....

....

....

....

....

....

....

....

....

....

....

....

....

....

....

....

....

....

....

You should spend about 20 minutes on this question.

Remember, this question is where you will also receive marks for your **spelling, punctuation and grammar**. So write and check your work carefully!

Make sure your answer stays focused on the question you have been asked and keep your answer relevant in a **sustained** way. Don't just write everything you know about the topic.

Links You can revise the Treaty of Versailles on pages 3–9.

This is a 'how far' question so you need to come up with a **balanced** response: ideas and evidence that support the statement, as well as points that do not.

Plan your answer before you start writing. List factors that support the statement in the question and list other factors that go against the statement.

Practice

Use this page to continue your answer to question 14.

....

....

....

....

....

....

....

....

....

....

....

....

....

....

....

....

....

....

....

....

....

....

....

....

....

It is a good idea to **signpost** your answer by beginning each paragraph with a clear statement to give the reader an idea of how the answer will develop. For example, 'The war guilt clause was very unpopular in Germany because …' and 'However, there were other elements of the Treaty of Versailles that were resented in Germany, such as …'

This will make it easier to write and will make your answer easier to understand. It will also show that you are developing **a clear line of reasoning** and show that you are considering **evidence** from both sides.

Practice

Use this page to continue your answer to question 14.

....
....
....
....
....
....
....
....
....
....
....
....
....
....
....
....
....
....
....
....
....
....

End your answer with a conclusion, giving a clear **judgement** about **how far** you agree with the statement in the question.

ANSWERS

Where an exemplar answer is given, this is not necessarily the only correct response. In most cases, there is a range of responses that can gain full marks.

SUBJECT CONTENT
Peacemaking
1. The First World War ends
The Germans requested an armistice to end the war, as they were unable to keep fighting and secure a victory. They hoped to keep some of the gains they had made, but the Allies refused to negotiate and Germany had no choice but to agree to their terms in order to stop the fighting. German civilians had suffered a great deal and there was widespread discontent because many were desperate for the situation to end. The German army had lost huge numbers of men. They were desperately short of the manpower and resources needed to win the war. After the USA joined the war, the Allies had more men and supplies, which meant that defeat seemed inevitable for Germany. By November 1918, parts of the German military were rebelling as they would not accept orders to fight battles that would end in failure.

2. The 'Big Three' and their aims 1
For example:
Similar:
- Both wanted Germany to be punished for the war.
- Both wanted Germany to be weaker militarily.

Different:
- Britain wanted Germany to regain its economic strength as a trading partner, but France wanted to ensure Germany was a weak neighbour.
- Lloyd George wanted Germany to be punished, but not weakened to the extent that Clemenceau wanted.

3. The Treaty of Versailles
Any three from:
- Germany's military was severely restricted.
- The Rhineland region was demilitarised to protect France.
- Germany lost territory, and was split in two by the Polish Corridor.
- The reparations imposed on Germany were punishing.
- Anschluss with Austria was forbidden.

4. The 'Big Three' and their aims 2
There is no right or wrong answer to this question. Any answer is acceptable as long as you give evidence for each of your reasons.

5. Reactions to Versailles: the Allies
For example:
- The British wanted Germany to be punished, and it was. The Americans wanted Germany to be punished less, and the French wanted it to be punished more.
- Wilson's Fourteen Points had been largely ignored – the policies of the freedom of the seas and self-determination would have been even more unpopular in Britain than in France.

6. Reactions to Versailles: Germany
For example, any three from:
- The terms were imposed on Germany without negotiation – it was a diktat.
- Germany had to take responsibility for the war, which was humiliating.
- Germany had to pay reparations even though its economy was in ruins.
- The restrictions on its military made Germany feel vulnerable.

7. The wider settlement
Any answer is acceptable as long as there is evidence for it. However, the 'usual' answer would be Turkey – they lost control of their economy and key trade routes, and had to allow Allied troops on their land, in addition to territorial losses and military restrictions.

8. The new states
For example:
- The new states were often created from a mix of ethnic groups, leading to tensions.
- The new states often shared borders with the countries which had once owned their land, which made them vulnerable to being taken back by them.

9. The treaty and fairness
There is no right or wrong answer here – you may argue that it was fair, or that it was unfair. The important thing is that you show that you have evidence to support your argument.

The League of Nations and international peace
10. League of Nations: origins
The goals of the League of Nations were to establish a new international order to preserve future peace. After the dreadful losses of the First World War, international leaders were determined to create an organisation whereby future conflict could be managed using peaceful methods of compromise and negotiation. The League wanted to protect the rights of member states to control their own futures without the threat of more powerful nations taking control. It also wanted to improve people's lives across the world by, for example, improving working conditions and tackling disease.

11. League of Nations: membership
The US Senate was worried the USA would get dragged into another European war by the League of Nations. It's surprising because it was President Wilson who had played such a key role in the League's creation.

12. League of Nations: organisation
Any two from:
- Arbitration could stop problems escalating and provide peaceful solutions. (effective)
- Sanctions were a peaceful intervention and if properly directed could be very effective. (effective)
- The Court of International Justice was an impartial body that could make binding decisions – an alternative to conflict. (effective)
- Moral condemnation was not an effective deterrent to aggressive countries. (not effective)
- Sanctions required everyone to act for the greater good, rather than in their own interests. (not effective)
- Military intervention depended on members agreeing to provide it. (not effective)

13. The League's agencies
There is no right or wrong answer here as long as you can back up your argument with evidence, and explain why the evidence is important. You should balance all the information and decide which achievements/failures were most significant. For example, think about:
- Which of the problems do you think were most important? A single really important achievement might outweigh a long list of minor ones.
- If there were failures, were they serious enough to cancel out the agency's achievements?
- Are any of the achievements made by the League's agencies still relevant today?

14. Peacekeeping in the 1920s
For example:
- In both the Åland Islands and Upper Silesia, the interested groups were willing to accept the judgement of the League of Nations.
- In both conflicts, the League of Nations managed to find a compromise position that the different sides found acceptable.
- Both conflicts were relatively minor in nature.

15. Diplomacy outside the League

For example:

- The Locarno and Kellogg-Briand agreements were viewed as major breakthroughs – but they had taken place without the League being involved.
- Diplomacy outside the League highlighted the problems caused by the absence inside the League of key powers – League discussions could not include the USA, Germany or the USSR, who were important global powers.

16. The Great Depression

For example:

- Countries became more inward-looking, meaning that they focused on their domestic problems and stopped thinking so much about the international picture. This made international agreements and collective security harder.
- The economic problems meant that some countries turned to nationalism to rebuild their countries. Many people believed the promises made to them by their dictators and supported their hostility to other nations' interests.

17. The Manchurian Crisis

For example, two from:

- The League of Nations appeared weak as it could not stop Japan's aggressive actions.
- Japan was a member of the Council, but it left the League rather than give in – this made the League look weak.
- The League found it impossible to reach prompt decisions about sanctions.

18. The Abyssinian Crisis

For example:

- Britain and France could have closed the Suez Canal.
- The League could have enforced sanctions on key resources such as coal and iron.

19. Outbreak of war, 1939

You can agree or disagree with the statement, as long as you give evidence for your reasons and explain why it was important.

If you argue that the failure was because of weaknesses that were there from the beginning, you could include two of:

- The absence of key powers meant that the League's ability to make effective agreements was limited – anything involving Germany, the USA or USSR had to be handled outside the League.
- The structure of the Assembly and the Council's power of veto made it hard to make decisions quickly.
- The lack of an army meant that taking military action against aggressive nations was very difficult.

If you argue that the problems were caused later, you could mention:

- The effects of the Great Depression made countries reluctant to impose sanctions on aggressive nations or send military to intervene, and hardened US isolationism.
- The aggression of Hitler and Mussolini was not the fault of the League – given how determined they were, it is unlikely the League could have stopped them.

The origins and outbreak of the Second World War

20. Hitler's aims

For example:

- The Treaty of Versailles was very unpopular with the German people – overturning it was seen as a step towards fairness.
- Hitler's policies would increase employment in a country suffering high unemployment.
- Many Germans were now living in other countries, due to loss of German territory caused by the Treaty of Versailles. Many people supported the reuniting of the German people.

21. Allied reactions to Hitler

For example, any three from:

- There was widespread fear of another war. France and Britain were still recovering from the First World War and the USA's policy of isolationism was driven by reluctance to be drawn into another conflict in Europe.
- Many people outside France were starting to feel that the Treaty of Versailles had been unfair.
- Some countries, for example Britain and the USA, thought that a strong Germany would protect against Stalin and the threat of communism.
- Governments were preoccupied with their own concerns, such as the rebellion against the government in France and the effects of the Great Depression in the USA.

22. The path to war

For example, any three from:

- attempting to renew the Anschluss
- introducing conscription
- expanding the Wehrmacht
- establishing an air force.

23. The Rhineland

For example:

- Reoccupying the Rhineland chipped away at the hated Treaty of Versailles, which Hitler had promised to overturn. This gained him support from the German people.
- It strengthened the border with France, allowing Hitler to pursue Lebensraum in the east without worrying about Britain and France attacking from the west.

24. Support for Hitler

For example, two from:

- Hitler's support of Franco in Spain provided the Nazi army and air force with experience in action and meant that Franco would owe Hitler support in return. Also, Spain shared a border with France, which was useful for Hitler.
- The Rome-Berlin Axis gave Hitler a key ally – Mussolini had opposed him at first, but now he knew Italy would not stand in his way.
- The Anti-Comintern Pact strengthened Hitler against a threat from the USSR in the east. If the USSR attacked Germany, it would risk Japan attacking the USSR's border with China.

25. Anschluss with Austria

For example, any three from:

- The Austrian army was added to German armed forces.
- Austria's natural resources were helpful to Germany's rearmament.
- It further damaged the Treaty of Versailles.
- It gave access to the east, vital for Hitler's policy of Lebensraum.

26. The Sudeten Crisis

Chamberlain's main concern was to avoid a war with Germany. He knew that if Hitler tried to take the Sudetenland by force, Britain and France could be obliged to go to war to defend Czechoslovakia. Hitler had assured him, and he believed, that if Hitler's demands were met in a peaceful and negotiated way, then he would be satisfied and war would be averted.

27. The Munich Conference

For example, two from:

- The USSR had not been consulted and this left Stalin angry and alienated.
- Hitler had increased confidence that he would not be challenged.
- The Munich Agreement was imposed on the Czechoslovakians without consultation, which led to anger.

28. Appeasement 1

Britain had suffered in WW1; people wanted peace. The country couldn't afford a war. People felt the Treaty of Versailles had been unfair.

29. Appeasement 2

You can argue that any of the arguments against appeasement is the strongest, as long as you can give reasons backed up with evidence and explain why the evidence is important. For example, if you chose 'The appeasers were wrong to believe Hitler when he said he was only interested in righting the wrongs of Versailles', you could say:

- Hitler had been saying since the 1920s that the only way to make Germany strong was to use military force – they should have been suspicious of his claims to want to avoid war.
- Hitler's huge rearmament programme and aggressive foreign policy did not fit with his claims that he posed no threat to his neighbours.

30. Invasion of Czechoslovakia

The Munich Agreement stated that Czechoslovakia would not be invaded. Chamberlain had been very keen to meet Hitler's demands as far as possible. The occupation of Czechoslovakia proved that Hitler's demands could not be satisfied and that he could not be trusted when he made a commitment. The people of Czechoslovakia were not German-speaking so Hitler's excuse of reuniting ethnic Germans did not stand up. Chamberlain finally accepted that Hitler had to be stopped in other ways.

31. The Nazi-Soviet Pact

- With Stalin agreeing not to intervene, there was nothing stopping Hitler invading Poland.
- The pact meant that Hitler knew it was safer for him to provoke the Allies, as they would not be able to count on support from the USSR.

32. Invasion of Poland

After the invasion of Czechoslovakia, Chamberlain had to accept that appeasement had failed and that Hitler would continue his aggression. Britain and France had promised to protect Poland so they were obliged to step in when Germany invaded.

33. Second World War: causes 1

For example, two from:

- The Great Depression meant that countries were more focused on solving their own problems, which meant that they were willing to undermine the League of Nations. This contributed to its failure.
- The terms of the Treaty of Versailles gave Hitler justification for his promises to rebuild Germany – by force if necessary.
- The poverty and unemployment caused by the Great Depression made people more willing to support dictators like Hitler, who promised jobs.

34. Second World War: causes 2

Long-term causes could include:

- resentment caused by the Treaty of Versailles
- the Great Depression making countries more focused on their own problems
- the weakness of the League of Nations
- Hitler's aggressive foreign policies having their roots in ideas he described the 1920s.

Short-term causes could include:

- the policy of appeasement encouraging Hitler to increase his demands
- Stalin's loss of trust in the Allies
- the Nazi-Soviet Pact removing the last protection for Poland.

The trigger was Hitler's invasion of Poland.

PRACTICE

47. Practice

The postcard shows a map of the 'Greater Germany' with Hitler's head positioned prominently in the centre. The message is that Hitler is dominating Europe and expanding into the areas around Germany to create an empire of German-speaking peoples. The date on the postcard is 13 March 1938, which was the day after Hitler invaded Austria, and one month before the plebiscite in Austria about the Anschluss. The map of 'Greater Germany' includes Austria.

The source is a postcard so could be displayed at home or work to show support for Hitler, or sent to friends or family. The slogan at the bottom of the postcard translates as 'One people, One Empire, One Leader', which gives a very positive message about Hitler's expansion and encourages people to support the Anschluss.

48. Practice

Both Sources E and F are useful for finding out about the formation of the League of Nations because they both deal with the origins of when the League was formed. The cartoon in Source E was produced in 1919 and shows President Wilson and a dove, symbolising peace. Wilson is giving the dove an olive branch labelled 'League of Nations'. This is referring to Wilson's belief that the League would be the way to ensure peace. However, in the cartoon, the branch is obviously too thick for the dove to carry, which means that the cartoon is saying that the League will not be as useful in keeping the peace as Wilson hopes. The size of the 'branch' might be a comment on the bureaucratic way the League was set up – that it was too awkward to help keep the peace. The cartoon is useful as it shows that even in 1919, some people were doubtful about how useful the League of Nations would be, even though the cartoon acknowledges that Wilson had good intentions.

The speech made by Wilson in Source F is useful as it shows his message to the world about the reasons why Germany was not allowed to join the League of Nations at that time. He says Germany 'ought to go through a period of probation' and prove that it had really changed before being allowed to join. It is useful as it shows the justifications that were used to decide who should be members of this international community. It also shows that President Wilson was willing to accept that Germany could be part of international cooperation, in contrast to the attitudes in countries such as France, who wanted Germany to be completely excluded.

However, there are some drawbacks with both sources for this enquiry. The cartoon in Source E is from a British magazine, and so it does not reveal anything about the attitudes of the other countries involved, such as France or the USA. For example, the US government refused to join the League, despite it being Wilson's idea. In addition, Wilson's speech was intended only to explain Germany's exclusion and says nothing about the aims of the League and how it would operate.

50. Practice

Economic problems after 1929 led to a range of problems for the League of Nations and contributed to its collapse. In 1929, the Wall Street Crash set off an economic emergency in the USA, and this led to a worldwide economic depression in the 1930s. The crash led to an economic downturn, which resulted in poverty and suffering in many countries. People had less money, so there was less demand for goods, which meant that international trade decreased.

As a result, many nations were increasingly hostile to each other. Hitler came to power in Germany and nationalist dictators took power in Japan and Italy. This meant that the League of Nations found it difficult to deal with international situations such as Italy's invasion of Abyssinia and the Manchurian Crisis.

The League had no army of its own, and member countries were reluctant to get involved in expensive military action during an economic downturn. Sanctions were another possibility but, with trade down, few countries were willing to refuse to sell their goods where they could. For example, only economic sanctions led by the USA would have real impact on the Japanese in Manchuria, but the USA wasn't a member of the League. When faced with a strong country which dismissed its rulings, the League of Nations appeared weak and useless. This undermined it further as an international organisation whose role was to police the world and resolve disputes as peacefully as possible.

The League was unable to stop the march to war in Europe in 1939 due to the lack of resources and political will of its member states.

52. Practice

Answers to Question 14 should:

- balance evidence to make a clear, logical argument
- give evidence that supports the statement and explain why
- give evidence that contradicts the statement and explain why
- make a judgement about which side of the argument is stronger – this is your 'how far'.

For example:

The Treaty of Versailles was widely resented in Germany for a range of reasons. The war guilt clause was particularly hated, but it was not the only aspect that led to the German public's resentment of the peace settlement. War guilt meant that the Allies felt justified in forcing the Germans to pay for the damage caused in the war in the form of large reparations payments. However, this was not the only reason why the German public resented the terms of the peace settlement.

The people of Germany were quite hopeful that the peace settlement would not punish Germany. Most Germans believed they had been forced into war and that all the countries involved should take responsibility. President Wilson had stated in his Fourteen Points that the future peace and stability of Europe was the most important aim of any peace settlement. Germany hoped that the Allies might want to give its new democratic government a chance to restore stability, but a harsh treaty would make it more difficult to do so. Wilson's ambition was to spread democracy around the world and therefore it made sense to give Germany's new government a real chance to succeed. Wilson was a key figure in the negotiations, and was keen to make the treaty fair because he thought that harsh terms would lead to German bitterness and a desire for revenge or another war in the future. When these hopes were crushed and article 231 stated that Germany had to accept war guilt, the German people were humiliated and angry and felt let down by the politicians negotiating the terms.

The war guilt clause was not the only reason that the Germans hated the Treaty of Versailles. The Allies had not even allowed the Germans to attend negotiations and now they were being forced to sign. However, the German politicians understood that Germany could not sustain any more fighting as the country and the people were in a desperate state, so unwillingly they accepted. The German representatives called the treaty a 'shameful diktat'. They said that Germany had been forced to accept terms that were unfair and deliberately humiliating. They also hated the treaty because it was imposed on them under threat of continued war. The decision to sign the treaty meant that many people in Germany were angry and said that they would do all they could to bring down the new government.

The German people felt that they were a strong and proud nation that the Allies wanted to weaken. The French concerns about security meant Germany's armed forces were severely reduced. The economic and psychological impact was very negative on the German people. They lost 10% of their land where around six million German citizens were living. So the Germans also hated the treaty because it weakened them economically and militarily.

In conclusion, the Treaty of Versailles was hated for many reasons. The war guilt clause 231 was an essential part of creating the resentment, but there were other important aspects of the settlement that they hated. The fact that the settlement was imposed on them and stripped them of land and resources and reduced their status as a nation were also important reasons for the deep level of negative feeling.

Notes

Notes

Notes

Published by Pearson Education Limited, 80 Strand, London, WC2R 0RL.

www.pearsonschoolsandfecolleges.co.uk

Text and illustrations © Pearson Education Ltd 2018
Typeset and illustrated by Kamae Design
Produced by Out of House Publishing
Cover illustration by Eoin Coveney

The rights of Sally Clifford and Victoria Payne to be identified as authors of this work have been asserted by them in accordance with the Copyright, Designs and Patents Act 1988.

First published 2018

21 20 19 18
10 9 8 7 6 5 4 3 2 1

British Library Cataloguing in Publication Data
A catalogue record for this book is available from the British Library

ISBN 978 1 292 20477 2

Printed in the United Kingdom by Bell and Bain Ltd, Glasgow

Acknowledgements
Content written by Rob Bircher, Brian Dowse and Kirsty Taylor is included.

The author and publisher would like to thank the following individuals and organisations for their kind permission to reproduce copyright material:

Photographs
(Key: b-bottom; c-centre; l-left; r-right; t-top)

Alamy Stock Photo: Pictorial Press Ltd 2l, Pictorial Press Ltd 2c, Sourced Collection 2r, Chronicle 11b, Granger Historical Picture Archive 16, Hi-Story 20t, Granger, NYC 24, World History Archive 26b, Shawshots 27, Pictorial Press Ltd 28, Keystone Pictures USA 29t, AF archive 29c, Everett Collection Historical 32t, Pictorial Press Ltd 32b, Chronicle 38, Chronicle 45, Photo 12 46; **Getty Images**: Past Pix 25, Library of Congress 29b; **Mary Evans Picture Library**: SueddeutscheZeitung Photo 37

All other images © Pearson Education

Note from the publisher
Pearson has robust editorial processes, including answer and fact checks, to ensure the accuracy of the content in this publication, and every effort is made to ensure this publication is free of errors. We are, however, only human, and occasionally errors do occur. Pearson is not liable for any misunderstandings that arise as a result of errors in this publication, but it is our priority to ensure that the content is accurate. If you spot an error, please do contact us at resourcescorrections@pearson.com so we can make sure it is corrected.